ESP and Personality Patterns

ESP *and*

Personality Patterns

BY GERTRUDE RAFFEL SCHMEIDLER

Psychology Department, City College of New York

AND R. A. McCONNELL

Biophysics Department, University of Pittsburgh

with an introductory note by

GARDNER MURPHY

GREENWOOD PRESS, PUBLISHERS
WESTPORT, CONNECTICUT

Library of Congress Cataloging in Publication Data

Schmeidler, Gertrude Raffel.
 ESP and personality patterns.

 Reprint of the ed. published by Yale University
Press, New Haven.
 Bibliography: p.
 1. Extrasensory perception. 2. Personality.
I. McConnell, Robert A., joint author. II.   Title.
[BF1171.S38 1973]   133.8   73-9258
ISBN 0-8371-6992-5

Reprinted with the permission of R. A. McConnell and
Gertrude R. Schmeidler

Reprinted in 1973 by Greenwood Press
A division of Congressional Information Service, Inc.
88 Post Road West, Westport, Connecticut 06881

Printed in the United States of America

10 9 8 7 6 5 4 3

Introductory Note

SUBSTANTIAL progress has been made in the last twenty years in the experimental analysis of paranormal phenomena. Utilizing the strict controls which are properly demanded today, investigators have gone beyond the sheer "demonstration" of such phenomena and have begun to study the psychological principles which underlie the capacity for extrasensory processes.

Dr. Gertrude R. Schmeidler is a clinical psychologist who has been doing pioneer research in this division of parapsychology. At Harvard in the fall of 1942 she began an examination of the relation between attitude toward extrasensory perception (ESP) and the actual ability to demonstrate ESP in a card-guessing task. In several large cycles of experimental work she found that those persons who believed in the possibility of ESP were able to score, on the whole, a little above chance expectation while those who disbelieved in it tended to score *below* expectation, with a difference achieving well defined statistical significance.

From this simple beginning she evolved at Harvard and later at the City College of New York a series of studies utilizing the Rorschach projective test and other well known psychological procedures to explore personality dimensions in relation to ESP performance.

She has been joined in this volume by Dr. R. A. McConnell, a physicist whose broad conception of experimental research and thorough application of modern statistical methods has greatly strengthened the presentation of these studies.

It has been my privilege to be associated with this research in a counseling capacity, and the progress represented by the appearance of this book is a source of personal satisfaction.

GARDNER MURPHY

Authors' Preface

WHEN a psychologist and a physicist find themselves collaborating on a book, they meet with problems; and the problems may become acute when, as in our case, they hope the book will be read by specialists in each field (and in other fields) and also by interested nonspecialists. To lighten the presentation, while keeping the rigor demanded by the subject matter, we have relegated to Appendix B the necessary exposition of the policies and methods followed in our statistical analyses. The serious reader could well begin with that appendix, and also with Appendix A, which presents a summary of the chronology and plan of the research.

Much more than this was needed, we discovered, to transform a controversial mathematical subject into pleasant armchair reading for the educated layman without alienating the scientist for whom the work is primarily intended. We have resorted to various simplifying devices in several parts of the book. Our embarrassingly numerous footnotes are intended to remove from the body of the text what is extremely simple and what is extremely complex; so that neither the specialist nor the beginner need be bored by what concerns only the other. In some cases where the climbing has been steep and the ascent unavoidable, we have segregated the mathematical discussion and suggested to the nonspecialist that he rejoin us at the top in the next chapter.

Throughout the book our findings are presented in numerical tables, intended to be intelligible without explanation to the professional user of statistical method. In our textual explanations of those tables we have allowed ourselves some looseness of expression. This is partly in the interest of brevity and style, and partly for the benefit of the reader who is not familiar with the analysis of variance. We hope that the specialist who wants to know exactly what hypotheses were under test will be able to make his own proper interpretation directly from the tables.

Co-responsibility should not necessarily be inferred from our use of "we." The data were gathered entirely by GRS and the statistical analysis has been primarily the responsibility of RAM;

at the interpretation and discussion we have labored jointly. In looking over the other's shoulder we have not always agreed, but we have hoped that each of our compromises will appeal to some readers without offending others.

The subject matter of the book divides into three parts. Chapters 1 and 2 are introductory, and 3 through 5 present our major findings. The remainder deal with preliminary findings, suggestions for further research, and the over-all picture. The professional scientist who, for one reason or another, wishes to scan the original experimental material in the book will find his need met by the summaries at the ends of Chapters 3 through 9 (see Table of Contents).

GERTRUDE R. SCHMEIDLER
R. A. MCCONNELL

September 1957

Acknowledgments

THE RESEARCH that is reported here, and the thinking behind that research, derive almost entirely from Gardner Murphy. It was Murphy who, in his seminar at Harvard, transformed GRS's vague curiosity about psychic research into a serious interest; it was he who initiated the first of these experiments by offering both funds and a basic hypothesis ("ESP arises in an unconscious, highly motivated state, free from conscious censorship")—a hypothesis incisive enough to be stimulating and yet general enough to leave to the experimenter the pleasure of working out the details. Through the years he continued to find the financial means for the research; and his encouragement when the work went slowly was vital in its continuation. His knowledge of the necessary experimental safeguards has helped to avoid pitfalls; his advice about the directions the research should take has largely determined its outline (it was he, for example, who suggested the use of both Rorschach and Picture-Frustration Study); and his insistence on the need for repetition and then further repetition has resulted in the accumulation of enough data to yield results that are statistically significant instead of merely provocative.

We gratefully acknowledge our further indebtedness:

To R. J. Snowdon, whose painstaking assistance to RAM in many phases of the manuscript preparation has hastened publication by a year.

To T. N. E. Greville and J. A. Greenwood, for their careful reading of our manuscript in the role of mathematical statisticians.

To J. G. Pratt and S. G. Soal who checked the accuracy of our reviews of their work in Chapter 2.

To the following instructors who lent their classes for the gathering of data: Ruth Berenda, Genevieve Chase, Rudolph Ekstein, Eugene Hartley, Rose Kushner, Gardner Murphy, Burke Smith, Virginia Staudt, William Triebel, Edith Wladkowsky, and Bohdan Zawadzki.

To Zygmunt Piotrowski and Bruno Klopfer, whose interpretation of Rorschach protocols is presented in Chapter 7.

To David Arbuse of Morrisania Hospital, who arranged for research with the concussion patients of Chapter 8.

To Christopher Scott and the (London) Society for Psychical Research, for permission to print his letters in Appendix C.

To Harvard University, which through Gardner Murphy as the Richard Hodgson Fellow financed GRS's research in parapsychology from December 1942 to June 1951.

To the American Society for Psychical Research, whose funds supplemented those from Harvard from January 1946 to February 1947.

To the A. W. Mellon Educational and Charitable Trust, whose encouragement and financial support made possible RAM's collaboration in this book.

Contents

Tables *

* See Table A-1 for chronological relationships.

CHAPTER 1

Introduction

To a research worker, nothing can be more challenging than an area of science which is almost unknown, which will contribute to basic theory in other better known fields, and which is of deep concern to human beings.

Such an area is psychic research. It is comparatively unexplored, potentially significant, and is closely related to psychology and psychiatry.

Despite a relationship to well established disciplines, psychic research (or "parapsychology," as it is more often called) is at present hampered in its development by the scarcity of trained people who are working in it. This book, which is composed chiefly of an account of our experiments, is being written primarily to enlist more investigators. Our hope is that the description of our findings will serve this purpose in two ways. The first is to demonstrate that the results of experiments tend to fall into meaningful patterns, and thus that productive research in parapsychology is possible. The second is to emphasize that important issues are still undecided, that certain techniques have been found particularly promising, that many problems require further study —and thus that a stimulating task awaits the worker in this new area.

There are several points that the reader might wish to see enlarged or defended before he reads about our experiments. Perhaps the most pressing questions are: Is psychic research actually a field of science? And is it important enough, either for other disciplines or for our personal affairs, to warrant utilizing the research time of trained people? We shall discuss these questions below and in the next chapter, before continuing with the account of our work.

One needs, first, to know when a body of material deserves to be classified as a field—or subfield—of science. The dictionary does not help us here, for a definition of science as "systematized knowledge of principles or facts" is too inclusive to satisfy many critics. They would require that the "knowledge" be obtained by procedures which are generally recognized to be the methods of science, so that they can examine the techniques used, as well as the "principles or facts" obtained through those techniques.

By such criteria, the history of psychic research as a science could probably be said to begin in 1882, when a group of scholars, most of whom were at Cambridge University, founded in London the Society for Psychical Research. Their methods, in their more ambitious undertakings, were at first those of the naturalist making field studies in some new area: they collected and analyzed the sort of anecdote that we all have heard, of ghosts and apparitions, of telepathic messages, of visions, premonitions, and so on. In these early exploratory studies their attitude resembled that of a lawyer cross-examining a hostile witness. They excluded all hearsay evidence. Whenever they could check the story by the accounts of others, or by reference to original records, they did so. Their findings, as far as possible, were published verbatim, so that the reader could evaluate for himself the contradictions, discrepancies, or corroborations of the material. Their reports still stand today as models of painstaking, critical research, within the limits of the field study technique.

Although some collections of new case material have continued to be made, and though they are both impressive and thought provoking, many of us are more stimulated than satisfied by such compilations. Eye witness accounts of flashes of lightning, no matter how well authenticated, do not give much understanding of electricity: we need also the less spectacular but better controlled researches of the laboratory. Thus, over the years, an increasing proportion of psychic research has been experimental. From the first simple attempts to study "thought transference" to the best ESP [1] experiments of today, control of conditions has

---

1. ESP, or *extrasensory perception*, has been defined by the *Journal of Parapsychology* as "response to an external event not presented to any known sense." The expression "not presented to any known sense" is to be taken broadly, including, for example, the idea of not capable of being inferred on the basis of past experience. *Telepathy* is the extrasensory perception of the "mental activities" of another person; *clairvoyance* is the extrasensory perception of objective events. All psychic phenomena are frequently subsumed under the term *psi*, used both as a noun and as an adjective.

been tightened and statistical evaluations have been refined, to the point where no serious criticism of the rigor of the methods can justifiably be made. (A few of the many well controlled experiments with positive findings will be summarized in the following chapter.) By the two criteria of using conventional scientific method and of obtaining systematized findings, parapsychology would at present seem fully to deserve being classified as a part of science.

The reader may well interject another question here. If the evidence is sound, why is not ESP generally accepted by scientists? One answer, though not a complete one, is that most of the experimental reports lie buried in technical journals with limited circulation. As an inevitable consequence of the large quantity of general scientific research that is published yearly, the research worker who should be concerned with the opening up of a new area is often not aware of it. On the rare occasions when he finds himself in a periodical library with enough time to browse, he will usually look for topics which he knows are close to his own inquiries. He is likely not even to see the two or three journals with unfamiliar titles that carry articles about the new field—though it may well be of great interest to him, after he becomes aware of its existence and its wider implications.

This brings us directly to our second question: the implications of parapsychology for other disciplines. One cannot foresee in detail the relationship of this field to others. But if history is to be trusted, the measure of the significance of a scientific discovery lies in the degree to which it seems to contradict established knowledge. ESP phenomena, such as telepathy or clairvoyance, are of a type that has no place in the physical universe —as modern physics has described it.[2] They show a contact with or response to distant events which no known force or radiation can explain. They seem to be unaffected by distance and intervening obstacles. There is evidence that they relate forward as well as backward in time. Psychokinesis, a cognate effect accepted by most parapsychologists, represents something that physicists have long assumed to be impossible: a direct response by a physical system to the wish of an observer. Since some or all of these phenomena do occur even though they "should not," we are forced to conclude that the picture of the universe which present-day

2. In another publication RAM [1956] has discussed the basis for this statement.

physicists have roughed out for us will have to be modified still once again, and that concepts of psychological ability will have to become broader than they are at present.

To touch briefly on the next point: what meaning can the known facts of ESP have for our personal lives? In one respect, very little, for most of the experimental findings are on too small a scale to give much promise of immediate utility. But even if we disregard the distant possibility of practical application, they still may have a good deal to offer. They reopen questions that had seemed closed, concerning the relationship of man to the world about him. If, as the data imply, our abilities somehow transcend the functions of muscles and known sense receptors, we can begin to speculate constructively about what the limits of transcendence are. Such problems as the efficacy of prayer, the possibility of survival after death, the feeling of being in contact with those we love, even when geographical distances separate us—these might now be considered questions for experimental investigation, questions which should not be dismissed out of hand. In one sense, the current fragmentary findings of psychic research show us only how ignorant we are; but the knowledge of our ignorance can be taken as a challenge or even as an encouragement. Given good research workers, we may reasonably hope that, later, more will be known and that science may be able to give us answers to questions which until now have seemed to lie outside of it.

Although we have been emphasizing the gaps between the data of psychic research and other research findings, there is one area where the conclusions drawn from ESP studies are largely consistent with what has been learned about other topics. This common area deals with the personality dynamics of ESP success and failure. It is noteworthy that although we do not know the means of communication between a subject and the ESP stimulus to which he is responding, and although we do not know what part of the body is sensitive to ESP stimuli, we have, nevertheless, learned something about the traits and attitudes which apparently facilitate or inhibit ESP response.

It is these problems of attitude and trait, the personality patterns of ESP success, with which this book is primarily concerned. Our approach will be the simple, positivistic one of searching for significant relationships between stimuli and subjects' responses.[3] Together with a description of procedures and findings, we shall present the tentative conclusions from our investigations and some ideas for further research. The work of others will be reported where it is directly relevant, but there will be no attempt to summarize all that has been done to relate ESP to personality variables.

3. In ESP, as in much of the research in perception, learning, etc., it may be possible to demonstrate such relationships even though we are ignorant of the intervening physiological variables. ESP research seems unique, however, in that in this area we are also ignorant of any intervening *physical* variables which permit the subject to react. It is as if we were studying the psychological responses to an experimenter's striking piano keys, before scientists had discovered the physical mechanism of sound transmission.

CHAPTER 2

Evidence that ESP Occurs

THIS CHAPTER is directed toward the person who is unfamiliar with psychic research. Our purpose in it is not to summarize all the research on ESP, nor to describe all the well controlled, careful research, nor even to describe that part of the well controlled research which offers important insights into the nature of ESP. All we hope to do here is to give the reader enough background so that he can accept ESP as a process that has already been established—a process just as real as vision, hearing, or learning, although less familiar than these and usually much less accurate. It is the contention of the authors that anyone competent to judge the authenticity of scientific findings, who is intellectually honest and has read the relevant material, must agree, however reluctantly, that ESP occurs. Here, then, is a summary of part of the relevant material.[1]

In 1919, at the University of Groningen (Netherlands), Brugmans, Heymans, and Weinberg [1922] performed a well planned experiment and obtained a remarkable result. They used for their major series only one subject, a student who in previous informal tests had seemed to show telepathic ability. The subject sat in a chair in front of a board which was marked off into squares of about two inches, making six rows and eight columns. Rows were designated by numerals; columns by letters. The subject's task was to find a particular square on this board. He made 187 trials. The target square was determined before each trial by one of the experimenters, who chose it by drawing a slip from each of two bags. One bag contained slips numbered from 1 to 6; the other contained slips lettered from A to H. Having drawn a slip

1. In another publication RAM [1957] has reviewed the evidence for ESP from a methodological point of view, and has discussed the relation of psi phenomena to several fields of science and the nature of the difficulties which have prevented the universal acceptance of these phenomena.

6

with a digit and another with a letter, he concentrated on the designated square.

The precautions taken by the experimenters to guard against sensory cues were various. Visual cues were avoided by blindfolding the subject and placing his chair within a large framework covered by black cloth on the top and on three sides. The back of the chair was to the open side. A small opening in the front permitted the subject's right hand and a part of his forearm to come through, so that his hand could touch the checkerboard. In approximately half the trials, auditory cues were prevented by an elaborate precaution. The experimenters' room was above that in which the subject sat. A hole was cut in the floor of the upper room, and two sheets of glass, with an air cushion between them, were put into the hole. The experimenters reported that this was sufficiently soundproof that shouts in the upper room could scarcely be heard in the lower one. In the other half of the trials the experimenters were in the same room as the subject, and attempted to prevent auditory cues by avoiding whispering.

In the standard procedure, six trials were performed with the experimenters in the upper room watching the subject's hand through the window in the floor. The experimenters then came down to the subject's room, changed the position of the board, and performed six more trials. In all cases the subject showed that he had chosen the position that he wished by making a double tap on the board with his forefinger. Only one of the experimenters knew which square was correct, until after the subject had made his choice.

According to statistical theory, an average of one trial in 48 should be correct, and one would thus expect about four correct responses in the total experiment. But the astonishing result was that there were 60 successes in 187 tries.[2] If one considers that

2. To anyone familiar with probability mathematics this result will indeed seem "astonishing." For others, an explanation is in order. The computed frequency of getting so high a score merely "by luck" is about one in 10^{50}, where the expression 10^{50} means one followed by 50 zeros. In most scientific work an isolated, anticipated result whose computed frequency of chance occurrence is one-in-twenty (a probability of .05) is considered suggestive of nonchance causation; while a result with a chance probability of .01 may be called "statistically significant." To say that a result is statistically significant means that it is considered to be substantial evidence of nonchance behavior.

there might have been some faint auditory cues with the experimenters in the same room, a slightly higher proportion of correct trials would be expected under this condition. But of the trials with the experimenters in the upper room, about 40 per cent were correct, instead of the expected 2 per cent; whereas, of the trials with the experimenters in the same room as the subject, about 30 per cent were correct. Both the magnitude of the scores and the pattern of the near misses show that the results cannot be explained in terms of uncertain scoring when the subject's finger was near the edge of a square.

There are some interesting sidelights on the experiment. One is that, for 29 of the trials, the subject took 30 grams of alcohol ten minutes before the experiment began. Twenty-two of these trials were successful. Another is that the subject's most successful efforts came when he was passive or relaxed, relaxation being determined by his own reports. In later work his galvanic skin responses were also recorded [1924].

Although the procedure used by Brugmans and his co-workers does not seem to have been employed elsewhere, impressive data supporting the ESP hypothesis have been obtained in other research, notably at Duke University by J. B. Rhine. In the course of his early investigations, which opened up a new period of ESP research, Rhine was (to give one example of his work) concerned with the problem of the relation between ESP success and the distance between the subject and the target. The question was investigated in 1933 under Rhine's direction, by J. G. Pratt, acting as experimenter, and Hubert Pearce, a student who had previously obtained high ESP scores, acting as subject [Rhine and Pratt, 1954].

The stimulus material consisted of decks of especially prepared cards, a variant of what are now usually called ESP cards. Each of the cards carried one of five simple, stylized symbols. The cards were arranged in decks of twenty-five, each deck including five of each of the symbols.[3]

3. These are designated as "closed" decks, in contrast with "open" decks. In an open deck there can be from 0 to 25 of any one of the symbols, since each position is filled independently of the others. When a subject guesses the order of the symbols in a closed deck, or when two closed decks are matched against each other, the "mean chance expectation" of successful guesses or matches is 5, with a "standard deviation" of not more than 2.04. With open decks the expectation is still 5, but

Decks were prepared for the experiment by careful, repeated shuffling, and then were cut. This minimizes but does not completely rule out the possibility of nonrandom order, which could affect the success of a guess. For example, in one of the decks a circle and a cross might stick together in repeated shufflings. If the subject has a tendency to "call" a cross after he has called a circle, he would then be more likely to have two "hits," instead of one, if the circle was guessed correctly. On the other hand, if he has a tendency to call a square after he has called a circle, he would be less likely to have two successive hits in the same situation. This gives rise to interesting statistical problems in evaluating the *standard deviation*,[4] but the *mean* number of hits to be expected by chance will not be affected. Experience has shown that theoretical considerations of this sort are of no practical consequence. For example, in the Pearce-Pratt experiment, the unimportance of card sticking—assuming that it occurred—was proved by control analyses which will be described below.

In those four series of the experiment where substantial distances separated the subject and experimenter (Table 1), the two men met in Pratt's office, compared their watches and made final arrangements, and Pearce left to go to the appointed place

TABLE 1. THE PEARCE-PRATT DISTANCE EXPERIMENT

DISTANCE BETWEEN SUBJECT AND TARGET	NUMBER OF RUNS (25 guesses)	DEVIATION FROM CHANCE EXPECTATION	MEAN HITS PER RUN †	CRITICAL RATIO
340 ft.	12	+ 59	9.92	8.4
740 ft.	44	+ 75	6.70	5.5
340 ft.	12	+ 28	7.33	4.0
340 ft.	6	+ 26	9.33	5.2
Total	74	+188	7.54	10.7

† *Chance expected value is 5.00.*

the standard deviation is exactly 2. The "mean chance expectation" is the simple arithmetical average of the card deck scores one would expect to get in a long series of experiments without ESP. The "standard deviation" is a measure of the scatter of those scores about their average value.

4. See n. 3, above.

for making his responses. After he had left the room, and after (in the three series conducted between the physics building and the library) Pratt had watched him from the window and seen him cross the quadrangle, Pratt shuffled and cut the cards. At a predetermined time he took the top card from the deck and laid it face down without having looked at it. One minute later he removed the next card from the deck, and so on, until the deck was completed. He went through two such decks in each session. After the session was completed, the order of the cards was recorded in duplicate by Pratt. One copy was put in an envelope and sealed before Pratt left the experimental room. The sealed envelope was submitted to Rhine. Pearce similarly submitted to Rhine a duplicate sealed record of his responses. Pratt and Pearce computed Pearce's scores from the records which they retained. Rhine made an independent computation from the duplicates in the sealed envelopes. The records were subsequently photostated.

There were 74 "runs" through the decks. Binomial theory gives an expectation of 370 correct responses; the number obtained was 558. This yields a "critical ratio"[5] of 10.7 and a corresponding chance probability of 10^{-22}.

In statistical work there are usually a number of analyses that can be applied to a set of data. All of these may be equally correct, although one, such as that just given, may be preferred for reasons of logic or precedent. The data of this experiment were chosen by Greenwood and Stuart [1937] for examination in diverse ways in order to illustrate mathematical techniques commonly used in ESP research. In the course of their work they carried out a control analysis in which the calls made at one experimental session were checked against the card order for the

---

5. The expression 10^{-22} means one divided by one-followed-by 22 zeros. Hence, 10^{-22} is a very small number.

A "critical ratio" is the number obtained in the next to the last step in certain statistical analyses. It can be converted directly into a probability value. For example, if a critical ratio of 2.5 is reached, it indicates that a score this far or further from expectation (in either direction) will occur by chance on an average of about once in 80 such experiments. Most standard probability tables go no higher than a critical ratio of 5, which is equivalent to a probability of less than one in one and one-half million for obtaining so extreme a score. When a still larger critical ratio is found, as in this Pearce-Pratt series or in the Brugmans experiment, a chance probability can be calculated, although it is obviously unreasonable to suppose that the data did, in fact, occur "by chance."

following session. The number of hits obtained in this way was 385, or 15 more than expectation—an insignificantly small deviation—and the standard deviation of the scores was found to be very close to the theoretical value. On the other hand, when they analyzed the calls against the intended cards by five different standard statistical methods, in every case the results were found to be extremely improbable on the chance hypothesis.

The highest average ESP scores ever published are described by B. F. Riess [1937]. Riess, an experimental psychologist, had attended a lecture on ESP given by Rhine, and reports that "training and interest in comparative psychology had made the author skeptical of the whole problem." He discussed it in his psychology class, where presumably his students were both less trained and less skeptical than he. One of the students volunteered to have a friend, who claimed to possess ESP ability, act as a subject in a series of tests. Riess accordingly performed an experiment with her, under conditions which he believed to be so rigidly controlled that, unless ESP really did occur, she would not be able to obtain successes other than those due to chance.

The subject lived about a quarter of a mile from him. She agreed to stay, while she made her responses, in a room which faced away from his house. He, acting as experimenter, remained in a room which faced in the opposite direction from her home. The possibility of sensory cues can therefore be disregarded.

The procedure was simple. Riess shuffled a "closed" [6] deck of ESP cards. At 9:00 P.M. on each evening that they agreed upon, he took the top card of the deck and noted it on a record sheet. At 9:01 he exposed the second card and recorded it, and so on, until the deck of 25 cards was completed. During the next ten minutes he prepared for the next run by shuffling the deck, and then repeated the procedure. There were two runs, or fifty guesses, at each session. The subject was instructed to guess at the cards at the time they were exposed. She returned her completed response sheets to the experimenter. Although she was curious about the scores she had obtained, she was not told what they were. Thirty-seven sessions were held. The subject then discontinued the experiment for three months, telling the experimenter that she had a "nervous breakdown." The first 37 sessions were called

6. See above, p. 8, n. 3.

Series A. When the experiment was resumed, thus beginning Series B, the subject participated in five sessions. She then moved to the Middle West and refused to take part in further research.

It is the data of Series A that deserve our attention. Out of 1850 responses, where chance expectation was 370 successes, the obtained number of successes was 1349. The average number of correct responses in each run of 25 guesses was 18.23, giving a critical ratio of 56.9 (Table 2).

TABLE 2. THE RIESS DISTANCE EXPERIMENT

SERIES	NUMBER OF RUNS (25 guesses)	DEVIATION FROM CHANCE EXPECTATION	MEAN HITS PER RUN †	CRITICAL RATIO
A	74	+979	18.23	56.9
B	10	+ 3	5.30	0.5
Total	84	+982	16.69	53.6

† *Chance expected value is 5.00.*

In Series B the subject reported that she thought she was scoring about as well as in Series A, but the experimenter tells us that she was less curious about the results. Here she made 250 separate responses, with a chance expectation of 50 hits. The number of hits obtained was 53, which is not significantly different from expectation. When the scores of the two series are pooled, the critical ratio of the total is 53.6, indicating that the probability of obtaining such results by chance is far beyond any reasonable possibility of coincidence.

Two critical comments about this experiment are frequently quoted. The first is that the subject may have falsified the results by entering Riess' home and changing his records. To this Riess gives two replies. One is that there was always a domestic in his home in those days, so that the possibility of the subject's making repeated surreptitious undetected entries seems absurdly far-fetched [personal communication to GRS]. The other is that examination of the records shows no signs of erasures or other changes.

The second criticism is offered by Riess himself. He was dissatisfied with his method because he had not studied the physiological and psychological changes in his subject during the two series, and thus could hardly make even an informed guess as to why there was such a sudden drop in her scoring level. Referring to the lack of supplementary data, he has written, in discussing the results, of "many uncontrolled factors." This remark was later misunderstood as referring to his precautions in collecting the data, and was taken as a reason for disregarding his work.

There is a third criticism, which we have heard but have not seen in print: the point that the experiment was unwitnessed, and therefore rests upon Riess' statement. Perhaps this kind of objection, which denies credence to a professional scientist's unverified word, can never be answered. It may, however, seem even less cogent when research is undertaken jointly by two or more experimentalists, as were the other experiments cited in this chapter.[7]

A more recent and important series should also be reported here [Soal and Bateman, 1954]. This consists of work done by S. G. Soal, an English mathematician, in collaboration with others. It was initially conceived as a rather routine project, an attempt to repeat the card-guessing experiments of Rhine and his co-workers under extremely rigid conditions. After testing 160 persons and collecting more than 128,000 separate responses, Soal concluded that his data showed no greater variation than would

7. Since this chapter was written, the question of experimenter honesty in ESP research has been dealt with openly in the leading journal of the American Association for the Advancement of Science. G. R. Price [1955], using an Aristotelian approach, has argued (a) that ESP is a priori impossible, (b) that the best experimental evidence for ESP cannot be explained away unless one assumes the dishonesty or insanity of the experimenter, and therefore (c) all experimental evidence for ESP that cannot be otherwise rejected is "dependent on deliberate fraud or mildly abnormal mental conditions." Dr. Price offered no evidence of fraud or mental disability in any modern experiment. He pointed out instead, that if enough co-experimenters and witnesses are willing accomplices, any experimental results can be fraudulently duplicated.

Further discussion in the same journal [1956: Bridgman; Meehl and Scriven; Price; Rhine (a, b); Soal; Wolfle] served to clarify some of the issues involved. Price has done a service for parapsychology, not only by his well documented presentation of some of the evidence for ESP, but also by his emphasis on the incompatibility between the experimental findings of ESP and prevailing beliefs in psychology and in physics.

be expected by chance. His results were well known in his own circle, and a fellow worker, Whately Carington, suggested (on the basis of Carington's own recent data) that they should be re-examined to check on the possibility that the subject's responses resembled the symbols before or after the intended target, even though they had only a chance relationship to the intended one.

Soal reports that after receiving a series of letters and post-cards from Carington, all making the same suggestion, he reluctantly began what promised to be a thankless task and was sure to be a tedious one. He found, however, that two of his subjects did in fact make exceptionally high scores on the card presented before the intended target card (that is, the [−1] position) and on the card presented after the intended target card (the [+1] position). He called these two subjects back for retesting, and found in 170 sessions, held over many years, producing thousands of responses, an extremely high scoring rate. We shall report in somewhat more detail on Basil Shackleton (BS), the first of these subjects, whose apparent penetration of the time barrier is still baffling to many of us.

The procedure that Soal chose to use in his follow-up series was unusual. The subject sat at a table with recording sheet and pencil before him and an observer with him. The subject was so positioned that if the door of his room had been wide open, he could not have seen through it into a second room to the spot where the experimenter, together with an "agent" and the target apparatus, were placed. (The door was left ajar to facilitate communication.) The target apparatus consisted of a large screen with a small window in it, set on a table. On the side of the table nearer the subject's room sat the experimenter (usually Mrs. Goldney, co-author with Soal of the most extensive paper on this work). She had two functions. One was to expose, through the window of the screen, a digit, taken in order from a previously randomized list. The other was to notify the subject that it was time to make a response, by calling "one," for the first response, "two," for the second, and so on.

Screened both from the experimenter and from the subject's room, the agent sat at the other side of the table with five cards before him. Each card was marked with a different one of the five symbols used as targets. At the beginning of each pair of runs he shuffled the five cards, then laid them face down in their newly determined order. If the experimenter showed through the window the digit 1, the agent picked up the card in the first position, turned it over, looked briefly at it, and then replaced it. Or for the digit 4, he looked at the card in the fourth position, and so on. At each verbal signal from the experimenter, the subject recorded his guess as to the symbol lying in the position corresponding to the digit. It is important to remember that the experimenter, who gave the signals and who was the only one who spoke, did not know what the correct symbol was. After two runs of 25 cards each, the correspondence between digits and symbols was recorded; for the next pair of runs a fresh symbol order was prepared, and a different list of digits was used.

Many further precautions were employed. There was usually at least one additional observer present. The observers and the experimenters were varied, so that a large number of reputable witnesses can vouch that the experiments were conducted as they were said to be. Duplicates of each session's results were made at the end of that session by the experimenter and the observers, and mailed in the presence of the members of the group to Professor C. D. Broad at Cambridge University. Records were checked, usually by four people. In some sessions the door between the subject's and the agent's rooms was kept closed; there was no change in the scoring level between these sessions and the others. Some sessions were held in rooms unfamiliar to the subject. Again there was no change in the scoring level. There seems to have been no reasonable possibility of fraud, sensory leakage, or statistical error in the major conclusions. And the most striking of the conclusions is that when the responses were scored against the symbol which was to *follow* the one on which the agent was concentrating, there were about 25 per cent more successes than would be expected by chance. The probability of such an average (for more than 11,000 guesses) is less than one in 10^{35}.

What does this mean? Was BS responding to an event that had not yet occurred? (This would be called "precognition.") Or was he responding—without being aware of it—to the next digit on the experimenter's list, and translating that digit to the appropriate card on the agent's side of the table? It will be remembered that at the time BS was responding, the agent could not see what the next digit was to be; nor did the experimenter know to what card the digit corresponded. And the observer who stayed with the subject ensured that the subject was always "in step."

Two procedural modifications were tried which ingeniously confirm the results and define more sharply the problem raised by the research. In one extended series with significant results, the order of the targets had not been randomly predetermined from mathematical tables. Instead, the experimenter dipped her hand into a reservoir of colored counters, picked one up without looking at it, and held it at the window. There were five colors, and the agent used them as he would digits, to designate the cards. Since BS continued his high ($+1$) scoring rate under these conditions, the simplest statement of the findings would be that he seemed to be responding to an event which had not yet occurred, and with an accuracy far above chance expectation.

In certain series the rate of calling was varied. When it was almost twice as rapid as usual (that is, one card in about 1.4 seconds, instead of one card in about 2.6 seconds), BS's scores fell to near the chance level on the target ($+1$) but rose to a high level on the target ($+2$). Thus, as before, he called the card that was to be designated about three seconds after his call was made.

Little comment is possible here on these remarkable results, except to refer the reader to the full account and to point out what must be clear already: that consistent results, under well controlled conditions, obtained by reputable research people, appear to have established facts which seem at the moment inconsistent with the great body of scientific knowledge. Insofar as they *are* facts, we can trust that they will eventually, by further research, be brought into congruity.

Not all ESP research is conducted with exceptional subjects. There are many good experiments, one of which will be described later in the chapter, where subjects consist of all those who volunteer. (Usually the ESP scores of unselected subjects are, at most, only slightly different from mean chance expectation, although, of course, the accumulation of many trials can make a consistent small effect statistically significant.)

A good reason for quoting the four preceding investigations— two of which involved distances of more than 100 yards between subject and target—was to make the point that repeated results with probabilities of this order of magnitude should not be expected to occur by chance in thirty-five years of research, considering the limited number of people who have done well controlled experiments in ESP. When a probability of 10^{-35} occurs in a single experiment with rigorously correct computation—an experiment, furthermore, that was expressly undertaken to retest previous, similar findings with the same subject—the chance hypothesis becomes untenable. And when other reputable investigators, also working under well controlled conditions, do research that results in comparably small probabilities, a strong case has been made for the occurrence of ESP.

Let us now return briefly to the problem of why so many scientists are still unconvinced of the reality of ESP. Limited repeatability and lack of theory are not in themselves sufficient grounds for rejecting a new phenomenon. Conversations with a sizable number of psychologists indicate that there are at least two other reasons for the prevailing skepticism on this subject. The first is ignorance of most of the research that has been done—regrettable but inevitable in an age of specialized science. The second is a feeling that flaws have been found in Rhine's experiments and that accordingly the whole ESP hypothesis is disproved.

Many of the early exploratory experiments were done under loosely controlled conditions. Critics of the work pointed this out, and argued that since certain of the findings could hypothetically be explained by sensory cues, or nonrandom targets, or arbitrary selection of cases, or scoring errors, rather than by ESP, parsimony of hypothesis required that they be explained in these several ways. At the American Psychological Association round-table on ESP methodology in 1938, many of these points were made very clearly. Each of them is a legitimate criticism of certain experiments, but they were sometimes stated so generally that they seemed to apply to all the experiments. There was only brief mention of the ESP results which could not thus be explained away. Thus the hasty reader, or careless listener, or the person with a second-hand account of the discussion, was often left with the incorrect impression that all previous work on ESP had been poorly controlled and was not worth consideration.

One of the consequences of these 1938 APA meetings was that certain psychologists who had expressed their critical interest in

ESP were invited to act as a Board of Review for the *Journal of Parapsychology,* where most of the ESP research in America was being published. Several accepted the invitation, and their comments on research were published along with the articles, for two and a half years. Of the experiments with tightly controlled conditions, where the report was approved without important reservations by the Board of Review, we shall describe only one. It was performed by Pratt and Woodruff [1939] and relates to a finding that has plagued parapsychologists. When a new procedure is used, subjects will often have ESP scores above mean chance expectation; but as they continue with that procedure the scores tend to fall. This leaves experimenters to wonder whether the first results were due only to chance, or whether the interest of a new procedure creates an attitude in the subject (or in the experimenter, which then affects the subject) that cannot be recaptured in later trials.

We shall describe in detail Series B in the paper by Pratt and Woodruff. They used as their procedure what has been called "screened touch matching." The subject sat at one side of a table on which was placed a large screen; in his hand was a pointer. Woodruff was seated at the other side of the table and handled the target deck of cards. The screen prevented the subject's seeing the card deck and any more of Woodruff than the top of his head. Pratt acted as an observer, sitting behind the subject.

There was an opening below the screen, two inches high and twenty inches wide. A baffle behind the opening on Woodruff's side blocked the subject's vision but allowed Woodruff to see the end of the subject's pointer. Above the opening, side by side, on five pegs on the subject's side, were hung five ESP cards, each with a different symbol. These "key" cards were visible only to the subject and to Pratt. The subject's task was to point through the opening, directly beneath the card which he thought was the correct one.

The experimental procedure for each run of 25 cards was as follows. While Woodruff shuffled and cut a closed deck of ESP cards, Pratt took the five key cards from the pegs and handed them to the subject, who changed their order and replaced them without giving Woodruff any indication of the new arrangement. After Pratt had resumed his seat behind the subject, Woodruff, holding the ESP deck face down, gave a ready signal. The subject then pointed beneath the key card which he thought corresponded to the card on top of the deck. Upon seeing the tip of the pointer, Woodruff placed the top card of the deck, still face down, behind the baffle and opposite the position of the key card to which the subject had pointed. Except that the ready signal was omitted, this procedure was continued with successive cards until 25 responses had been made.

The official recording was done on two data sheets, previously prepared with identical serial numbers. Using one of these sheets, and with the screen left in position on the table, Woodruff turned over the cards and recorded the actual distribution of the 25 cards. Meanwhile, Pratt, using the other data sheet, recorded the order of the key cards, the name of the subject, the date, etc. These two data sheets were then clipped together and without further ado, dropped into a locked record box. The keys to this box were in the sole possession of a secretarial assistant.

The unofficial counting then took place. The screen bearing the key cards was tipped on its side and Pratt, with the others looking on, sorted the hits from each pile, laying them nearer the key cards and counting aloud the number of hits in the run. After a recounting, this score was immediately recorded by each experimenter in his personal record book for later checking against the official records, after they had been independently scored by the secretarial assistant.

For a full description of the precautions taken the reader must refer to the original paper. Because of the many experimental and statistical controls that were used, it seems safe to say that no statistical demonstration in ordinary psychology has ever matched the rigor of this Pratt and Woodruff experiment. Since its publication there has been no known attempt to criticize it in print.[8]

The standard size ESP symbol is about 1½ inches. In this experiment, in addition to the standard size, three other sizes were used; namely, $\frac{1}{16}$ in., $\frac{1}{4}$ in., and 2¼ in. The experimenters comment that when they showed each new stimulus size to the subject, and told him that it was to be his next target, they generally

8. Since this statement was written an inappropriate criticism has appeared [Soal & Bateman, 1954, p. 56] arising from the critic's failure to read carefully the original research paper [see McConnell, 1954, p. 252].

phrased their instructions so as to challenge him to score better than before. There are, then, three points to examine. Was there evidence of ESP? Was there a relation between stimulus size and scoring success? And was there a relation between experimenter's challenge and scoring success?

The answer to the first question is unambiguous. In 2400 ESP runs of Series B, above described, there were 489 more hits on the target than mean chance expectation. After all possible corrections have been made, these results are found to have a chance probability of one in 500,000.

As to the second question: no significant relationship between stimulus size and scoring success was shown, either in Series B or in the experiment as a whole.

And for the third question: there was a substantially higher scoring rate on the new targets than on the old ones. On targets that had been used in previous series the average score was 5.09 for each 25; on the new targets the average was 5.33. The difference between the two is statistically significant with a probability of less than .001, for the paper as a whole. Thus, under carefully controlled conditions, with subjects chosen in terms of their readiness to volunteer, the experimenters not only demonstrated that ESP occurred, but also that the psychological conditions of the experiment were related to its occurrence.

CHAPTER 3

The Initial Experiment: Separating the Sheep from the Goats

IN VIEW of the published data supporting the ESP hypothesis, it may seem surprising that, when beginning her own experiments, GRS approached the problem without conviction. She cannot defend on intellectual grounds this reluctance to believe the evidence. In spite of having read the material with a critical attitude, searching with care for uncontrolled conditions or inadequate treatment of the data, she had been unable (in many cases) to find any weakness of consequence. This hesitation in accepting conclusions derived from good research with clear-cut findings (a hesitation which some readers may share) was due, of course, to the conflict between those conclusions and her own assumptions. To open the door to telepathy or clairvoyance meant re-examining basic concepts; and the process was sure to be so difficult and so uncomfortable that she put it off as long as possible.

The first experiment was undertaken in 1942 almost as if it were a wager made with herself: if extra-chance results were obtained from conditions which she knew at first hand to be impeccable, then she would resign her emotional opposition to the ESP hypothesis. And such results were obtained.

The arrangements for the first experimentation were as follows: [1]

Subjects. To be chosen "at random." In practice this meant asking acquaintances in the Harvard Psychology Department to act as subjects, and calling for volunteers from certain of the Harvard and Radcliffe elementary psychology classes.

Stimulus Material. The standard ESP cards, arranged in the usual decks of 25 were used because they facilitate comparison

---

1. The procedure was modified slightly when beginning the first formal experiment (below, pp. 24–27) and again for series 4–7 (below, pp. 32–33).

with the results of other workers. The decks were to be "open" (see above, p. 8, n. 3). They were to be arranged in the following manner: A paid assistant would make a private and arbitrary list in which two digits would be assigned to each of the five ESP symbols. She would then enter at random a table of random numbers [Peatman and Schafer, 1942; Tippett, 1927]. She would note the point at which she entered the table, and would record lists of symbols by following the digits in the table according to some such system as reading down the columns, or reading across the rows from left to right, or reading up the columns. She was to treat each list of random numbers as circular, and when she returned to the starting point, continue according to some other system which she had not previously used. The lists of symbols were to be written on serially numbered sheets. Next, decks of cards, numbered to correspond with the sheets, were to be prepared following the same stimulus order. The cards were to be slipped into opaque containers, and the lists covered so that they were not in sight. The experimental room was to be kept locked both while she was making up the lists and after she left. The assistant was to tell no one, not even the experimenter, what the order of symbols was.

Experimenter. GRS was to act as the only experimenter.

Procedure. The assistant was not notified of what subjects were to be tested, or of how many subjects were scheduled for any day, or of how many lists each subject would use, so that if she wished to give them advance information she would not be able to do so. (There was no evidence that such caution was necessary; but since the assistant evinced no interest in finding which subjects were to be tested, keeping the information from her was a part of the normal routine.)

Two rooms, separated from each other by intervening rooms and a corridor, were employed. The subject used one; the cards and target lists were in the other. The shortest distance from the subject's chair to the cards was 42 feet, on a line which passed through the walls of two other rooms and the corridor. The rooms were connected by an electric system which activated a buzzer or light in one room when a telegraph key was depressed in the other. This was used to signal the beginning or end of a test series.

The experimenter ushered the subject into the room in which he was to make his responses, explained something of the nature of the experiment to him, and gave instructions as to the procedure. The only information about the location of the cards was that they were "on top of the pile" in another room. The subject's comments and behavior were recorded. The experimenter then went to the other room, while the subject filled in the 25 blanks on a record sheet, numbered to correspond with the appropriate stimulus list. The experimenter remained there without having looked at the target. Thus, in the initial experiment, as in all of the later work except as specifically noted, the test was of an ostensibly clairvoyant type. The experimenter did not know the cards at the time they were guessed, although their order had been seen by someone when they were prepared.[2]

When, in this first standard procedure, the subject pushed the signal key, the experimenter took the target list to the subject's room and checked it against the subject's responses. If the subject was willing to make another run, the procedure was repeated with the next target list. There was a maximum of ten runs in each session, and the maximum length of each session was one hour. All responses were independently rescored later by the assistant, and discrepancies were checked.

The first few subjects that were tested scored slightly better on the hidden targets than the chance rate of one success out of five. Graduate students, interested in the research, they had expected the over-all results to be better than chance expectation. The next subjects, two psychologists, expressed a very different attitude. They said that the experimenter was wasting her time by trying to find out about ESP, and they tacitly indicated that the sooner the results were so poor that the investigation could stop, the better it would be for all concerned. One of these two subjects said

2. From a logical point of view there are other possibilities beside the obvious one that information traveled directly from the cards to the brain of the subject (clairvoyance). To cite three examples, the information might have come from the thoughts of the assistant as he made up the card list (retrocognitive telepathy), from the memory traces of those thoughts (telepathy or clairvoyance, depending upon the definition), or from the future thoughts of the experimenter as she inspected the card list (precognitive telepathy). Although this kind of theorizing has occupied the attention of some parapsychologists, it need not, in view of our present experimental ignorance, concern us further here.

that her mother and grandmother had believed that they were psychic, and that she would be pleased when everyone agreed that such a contention was absurd. The other based his opposition to the research on theoretical grounds. ESP, he said, was inconsistent with behaviorism; and he was a behaviorist. He was discussing the general question one day after lunch, and GRS asked him what he would think if the data turned out to show that ESP occurred. His answer closed the discussion. He laughed, tilted his chair back, puffed at his pipe, and said, "If it were true, I wouldn't believe it!"

In spite of their disapproval of the concepts behind the research, these two psychologists were willing to act as subjects. Both scored fewer successes than would be expected by the chance rate of one out of five. The juxtaposition of their low scores with the higher ones of the subjects with a favorable attitude toward the experiment led to a hypothesis about ESP: that subjects with a favorable attitude toward the experiment would make higher scores than those with an unfavorable one.

This marked the end of the exploratory work. (These fragmentary, preliminary data are not tabulated in this book.) In beginning the first formal experiment, one basic modification was introduced into the procedure just described. During an initial chat, and before they had made their first ESP response, subjects were categorized as either accepting the possibility of ESP under the conditions of the experiment, or as rejecting any possibility of ESP under these conditions. What this amounted to, in practice, was that those whose expressed attitudes were favorable, or hopeful, or interested, or even hesitant were put into the former category; those who expressed themselves as being firmly convinced that there could be no paranormal success under the conditions of the experiment were put into the other. (It is to be noted that the hypothesis being tested by this two-class division of subjects was narrower than the one that had been first formulated.) [3]

3. The subjects who accepted the possibility of ESP under the conditions of the experiment were called "sheep"; the others were called "goats." In retrospect, the problem of defining these terms seems less simple and more important than it did at the beginning of this research. In the early reports, which cover the individually tested subjects of this chapter and the next, the matter was discussed in a casual and possibly misleading fashion, particularly as regards the phrase "in the experimental situation." A question raised here by RAM is whether a subject who accepted

Having thus "separated the sheep from the goats" according to whether or not they accepted the possibility of paranormal success in the present experiment, an attempt was made to sharpen the difference between the two groups by making the experimental conditions more agreeable for the former than for the latter. This involved minor procedural changes for each group. For the "sheep," the changes consisted of having cigarettes available for them throughout the session, of sometimes offering them candy, and sometimes, when the weather was warm, offering them a carbonated drink.

For the "goats," two changes of a different sort were introduced. The first was that the external surroundings were less pleasant. This was accomplished by reversing the two experimental rooms. Targets were placed in the airy corner room where the sheep made their responses, and each goat made his responses in the rather shabby and poorly lit darkroom where the sheep targets were kept. The pencil provided for making responses was only a stub; the surface of the table on which he wrote was battered. None of the goats commented on any of these points; and it was the experimenter's impression that they either did not notice them, or else took them for granted as normal in any experiment.

The second change in procedure was that the goats were not permitted to see their scores at the completion of each run. This speeded up the experimental procedure so markedly that it was

---

the possibility of paranormal success under some conditions, but not under the conditions of the experiment, would have been classed (incorrectly) as a sheep.

To tie down the historical facts as objectively as possible, GRS has searched her interview notes of the earliest work. Those show that in the first of the three series reported in this chapter there was one subject who accepted the possibility of telepathy but not of clairvoyance and who was (correctly) classified as a goat. This fact and a critical reading of the published papers indicate that the restriction "in the experimental situation" was applied from the beginning of the research, to the extent that the informal questioning methods used with the individually tested subjects supplied the necessary information.

Another ramification not appreciated in the beginning was the possibility that a subject might believe that, although others could employ ESP in the given experimental situation, he himself could not. By definition, such a subject is a sheep. Examination of interview notes shows that all subjects who stated such beliefs were (correctly) classified as sheep.

The total number of subjects affected by these uncertainties would be small, and we judge that the resulting uncertainty in the operational meaning of the findings is negligible. (The *complexity* of psychological meaning in the sheep-goat dichotomy is dealt with hereafter, especially in Chapter 6.)

possible to set a maximum of fifty runs in the hour-long session. Since fifty separately numbered slips of paper might well have led to confusion, the goats were required to record their responses on large record sheets, each of which held eighteen columns. A further modification of the procedure followed on this one. After instructions were given, the experimenter went to the room in which the targets were kept and, without looking at the target list, pressed the telegraph key which sounded a buzzer in the subject's room. This was the signal that the subject was to begin his responses to the first list. When he completed them, he pressed a key which signaled in the experimenter's room. The experimenter then put aside the first deck, leaving the second deck on top of the pile, again without having examined it, and sounded the subject's buzzer as a signal to begin the second list. This was continued until fifty target decks—or symbol lists in lieu thereof— were completed, or until the hour was done.[4]

Although there were individual variations in scores, the over-all data of these first subjects were clearly in the direction suggested by the hypothesis. (See Table 3, Series 1, page 33.) When the difference between ESP scores of sheep and goats had reached the .03 probability level of significance,[5] it was decided to begin a second series of subjects.[6] The second series was to include, as nearly as possible, the same number of subjects and the same number of runs as the first series; and the subjects were to be tested under the same conditions. Their results were roughly similar to those of the first series. A third series was then instituted, and again the attempt was made to keep the experimental conditions, the number of runs and, so far as possible, the num-

---

4. Among all the individually tested subjects (Chapters 3 and 4) two sheep (in the series designated as 2 and 3) requested that a testing procedure be used that would allow the experimenter to think of each card. This was done for 25 card guesses with each of these subjects, yielding in both cases a score of three correct guesses. For these cases the subject pushed the signal key after each guess, thereby telling the experimenter to look at the next card.

5. Approximate value using binomial theory with a card probability of one in five. For a full analysis see the following chapter.

6. The termination of an experiment upon reaching a given level of significance is frowned upon by mathematicians who are concerned with the use of statistical method as a *logical* tool. This procedure is nevertheless frequently appropriate for the investigator to whom statistical method is an *experimental* tool. For a discussion of "optional stopping" as applied to these data, see Appendix A.

ber of subjects, the same as in the other series. When this series, which also gave similar results, was completed, it was found that the pooled data of the three series showed a difference between average ESP scores of sheep and goats which was at the .005 level of significance. It therefore seemed wasteful to continue with further repetitions without modifying some of the variables.[7] These three series constituted the initial experiment [Schmeidler, 1943a, 1943b].

Let us consider it in more detail. It may be said that the function of an experimenter is to formulate a hypothesis and to collect and report data bearing on that hypothesis. From this point of view the experiment, as described above, had been completed— and to the extent of the odds against chance, it did serve the purpose of convincing the reluctant experimenter, if no one else, that the ESP phenomenon occurs. Most research workers would agree, however, that an experimenter should do more than test hypotheses; he should also examine the subject's behavior and the pattern of his scores in order to obtain hints for new hypotheses. It therefore seems appropriate to report here further observations and impressions, which in some cases formed the groundwork for later research and in other cases represent loose ends that still need investigation.

Of the undergraduates who acted as subjects, the boys seemed to make higher ESP scores after they had had something to eat or drink; many of the girls seemed to make higher scores after they had been given an opportunity to talk about themselves. The unfortunates with examinations scheduled for later in the day did not score many successes. The students who gave the impression of being earnest, shy, and self-conscious made somewhat lower scores than the others. The cumulative effect of these and other similar observations suggested that it would be profitable to make a systematic study of personality patterns in relation to ESP success. The description of such studies makes up the greater part of this book.

The reader may be interested in thumbnail sketches of some of the subjects whose scores and personality patterns seemed to be internally consistent, although they were very different from each other. One, whom we shall call A, was a girl who expressed keen

7. See above, notes 5 and 6.

interest in the experiment but averaged only three successes per run. She returned for another session, saying that she ought to do better this time, and that previously she had been worried about a test she was about to take. Her score average for her second visit was near to seven hits per run. In some later sessions, which were considered to be independent and exploratory, not a part of the major experiment that was being conducted, it was usual for A to make her ESP guesses verbally while she was finger painting, and for the experimenter to be present in the experimental room, recording her guesses, other comments that she made, and notes on her behavior. Interviews revealed that she was gifted and volatile, with abilities that were above the average in many lines, none of which had been fully developed. Her moods showed marked variation; her ESP scores seemed to vary with her moods; and her finger paintings to symbolize those variations both in color and form. In one session, for example, her first two paintings were of dark clouds under water, and her ESP scores were below chance expectation. Her third painting was done quickly with bright colors, and went beyond the limits of the paper, onto the board to which the paper was tacked. Conversation revealed that it expressed overt aggression against her father. During this period of release her ESP scores were above chance expectation. During a series of guesses she would sometimes comment that she thought she was doing well—or badly—and the comments were usually correct. She reported a dream which she had had in the previous year which seemed to be paranormal. The over-all pattern gave the impression of unusual ESP ability which she could not control deliberately, but which she could recognize while it was functioning, and which in her happier or freer moods showed itself by hitting the target, in her depressed moods by avoiding the target, although her conscious volitional pattern seemed to her to be the same no matter what her mood.[8]

8. The Harvard and Radcliffe undergraduates who made up the bulk of these early subjects were a highly articulate group and gave rich introspective material, but there was little or no relationship between introspective report and ESP success. Some subjects checked guesses about which they felt confident; some reported visual, auditory, or kinesthetic imagery; some described the ease or difficulty of their responses; but only in the case of A was there any hint of a consistent pattern that related to ESP. No further study of such introspective material has been made in this research.

Another subject, B, was something of a professional dilettante. In early middle age he was still studying in a university, and he had been studying in various universities for most of his adult life. As soon as he approached competence in one field he shifted to taking courses in another field; he knew enough about a great many topics for brilliant, showy conversation, but not enough for critical or creative scholarship. He had had some striking experiences which seemed to be paranormal, and was proud of them. When he heard that an ESP experiment was being conducted, he asked if he might act as a subject "to see if I can make a good score." As the procedure was being explained to him it began to be clear that he meant literally what he had said: he wanted to show that he could make a single high score. On the eighth run his score was 12 hits, which is well above chance average, but not unusual in a long series of tests. He made one more run, but could not be persuaded to complete the ten runs which made up the usual session. The average of the nine runs he completed was 5.4, which is not unusually high. He seemed, in the ESP experiment as in his total life pattern, to be satisfied with a spectacular but transient achievement.

A third subject, C, was a young woman who had great zest for anything that seemed like fun and that offered her a change, but who also appeared to be unsure of herself. She gave the impression of reaching out to adventure and then pulling back to safety. During the time that the experimenter knew her she accepted a responsible but poorly paid position and was extremely competent at it; but she left it after a year to take another position which was at least as difficult and offered even less security. She married impulsively a man whom she hardly knew, and was separated from him after only a few weeks. When first asked to act as an ESP subject she was delighted with the idea, arranged an appointment readily, entered into the spirit of the experiment to an unusual extent, and seemed to enjoy herself. (She asked that the shades be drawn so that she could relax, and with the experimenter made elaborate arrangements and rearrangements of the chair and table so that she could write her responses more readily.) Her average score for the ten runs was outstandingly high. A short time later she was asked to have another try at it so that we could see if she had real paranormal ability. She agreed to this proposal without enthusiasm, acted as a subject only after repeated requests, and had an average score for the second session which was slightly below chance expectation.

At that time, the drop in score seemed puzzling. The experimenter had accepted provisionally the hypothesis that ESP scores indicated the level of a subject's ESP ability, and thus expected that, chance variations aside, a person who did very well in one session should do well in the next session too. Now, though perhaps it is only being wise after the event, C's low scores in her second session seem a natural sequel to initial high scores. Both in her marriage and in her work she had entered a new field with great enthusiasm and with initial success. But she turned away from both as if she were unwilling to make long-term achievements, and in the same way she seemed half afraid of ESP *after* she had done so well at it as to imply that she might have unusual paranormal ability.

This girl's behavior illustrates a psychological principle that seems to be of special importance in parapsychology. The ego-involvement that comes from an initial participation can make marked changes in a subject's approach to the repetition of a task, even though his verbal statements about his approach remain unchanged. In consequence, it is perhaps not to be expected that subjects will give similar results in succeeding test sessions. This should be especially true if the subject learns his score as the testing proceeds.

Summary of the Initial Experiment

Subjects were required to make ESP responses under rigidly controlled conditions. Before making his first ESP response each subject was categorized as either a "sheep" or a "goat." The sheep were subjects who accepted (though sometimes with reservations) the possibility of paranormal success under the conditions of the experiment; the goats were subjects who rejected this possibility. In this first experiment the experimenter attempted to make the testing session more agreeable for the sheep than for the goats. In three successive series the average ESP score of the sheep was higher than that of the goats. When the three series were pooled, the difference between the means of the two groups was found to be statistically significant with a chance probability of about .005. The statistical analyses of these and similar data are given in the following chapter; the relation of these data to all of the experimental work of the book is set forth in Table A-1, below, page 112.

CHAPTER 4

Further Tests of Individual Sheep and Goats

FROM a full analysis of the three series described in the preceding chapter, one point was established with reasonable certainty: two groups of subjects who could score at different levels of ESP had been separated from each other. The major difference between the two was presumably that of acceptance or rejection of the possibility of paranormal success under the conditions of the experiment—but this was only a presumption, since there were other obvious differences between the two groups (number of runs per session, knowledge of score after each run, interior decoration of the experimental room, perhaps more warmth in the experimenter's response to the "sheep," etc.). In the next four series many of these differences were controlled and, as will be seen, the sheep-goat effect persisted.

As implied in the last chapter, the emphasis of the research shifted, after the first three series, from a contrast of sheep with goats to an analysis of personality factors involved in ESP scoring. There was no effort, in any later series, to make the goats less comfortable than the sheep. The procedure already described for testing the sheep was followed, in all essentials, for both sheep and goats of the four further series of individual tests. There were the following minor changes. All subjects were required to make nine runs. To save time, subjects were instructed to make three runs without interruption. After each series of three runs the responses were scored. There was a short break between successive sequences of three runs, which was filled with a short projective test, or with conversation, or both. A further change, necessitated by a removal from the Harvard Psychological Laboratory to the Harvard Psychological Clinic for the fourth, fifth, and sixth series,[1] and to the rooms of the American Society for Psychical Research for the seventh series, was that the target lists were kept

1. The distinction among the fourth to sixth series was primarily chronological.

in a closed closet or a closed drawer instead of in a separate room. The experimenter stayed with the subject while he made his responses, busying herself with other work, and was ignorant of the stimuli in the target list until the subject's responses were completed. Some of the subjects in the seventh series were paid a small sum for taking part in the experiment.

The results for all individually tested subjects are shown in Table 3. The difference between sheep and goats for all series combined is significant with a chance probability of .000,06. The scores from the later series are so similar to those of the earlier as to make it seem unlikely that the special conditions imposed

TABLE 3. ESP SCORES OF SUBJECTS WHO WERE TESTED INDIVIDUALLY BY SCHMEIDLER. A COMPARISON OF SUBJECTS WHO ACCEPTED THE POSSIBILITY OF PARANORMAL SUCCESS UNDER THE CONDITIONS OF THE EXPERIMENT (SHEEP) WITH SUBJECTS WHO REJECTED THIS POSSIBILITY (GOATS) †

ACCEPTANCE ESP OF	SERIES	NUMBER OF SUBJECTS	NUMBER OF RUNS (*25 guesses*)	DEVIATION FROM CHANCE EXPECTATION	MEAN HITS PER RUN ‡
Sheep	1	12	129	+ 56	5.43
	2	12	127	+ 33	5.26
	3	22	133	+ 31	5.23
	4	9	162	+ 34	5.21
	5	23	207	+ 45	5.22
	6	19	171	+ 27	5.16
	7	14	126	+ 16	5.13
	Total	111	1055	+242	5.23
Goats	1	4	200	− 10	4.95
	2	4	175	− 13	4.93
	3	4	199	− 11	4.94
	4	3	54	− 41	4.24
	5	3	27	− 23	4.15
	6	16	144	− 26	4.82
	7	6	54	+ 8	5.15
	Total	40	853	−116	4.86

† *The procedure for series 1–3 is given in Chapter 3 and for series 4–7, in Chapter 4.*
‡ *Chance expected value is 5.00.*

upon the first twelve goats need be considered further. If anything, the goats showed a stronger avoidance of the target under
the objectively pleasant conditions of Series 4–7 than under the
objectively unpleasant ones [2] of Series 1–3. The data suggest that
the factor of belief or acceptance was somehow of crucial importance to the ESP scoring of these subjects.

The remainder of this chapter will be devoted to a mathematical examination of the data thus far reported. The reader interested solely in the psychological findings may wish to skip to
page 42.

There are usually many tests of significance that can be applied
to a given group of experimental data. Opinions might differ as
to which test, if any, is the most appropriate. Different workers
will emphasize differently such criteria as simplicity, precedent,
and generality. Certainly, there are legitimate differences in the
objectives for which mathematical analysis can be employed. Some
of our readers may prefer that we present only a conservative
minimum of established knowledge, because the area is still controversial. Others may feel that it is equally important to extract
by every proper means any clues that can point to future dis-
coveries.

The method we have chosen for general use in this book is the
analysis of variance. The considerations leading to this decision
are more fully explained in Appendix B. Briefly, we believe that
this method provides a maximal combination of rigor and flexi-
bility: it will serve the purposes of the greatest number of our
readers.[3]

2. It is not unlikely that if the unpleasant surroundings or the dull procedure
had been perceived as disagreeable, they would have had an adverse effect on the
results. But the subjects' reports, both spontaneous and after questioning, as well
as their behavior, indicated that when they agreed to act in an experiment they
tended to disregard their physical surroundings, and also that they considered the
50 uninterrupted ESP runs as dull, but not excessively dull, in terms of their expectation of experimental procedure.

3. For the reader who is not familiar with analysis of variance but who wants
to follow our presentation as far as possible, the following explanation may be useful.

Throughout the book, wherever the mathematical term "variance" occurs, sub-
stitute "scatter," which is a loosely equivalent nontechnical word. If chance alone
is operating, card-guessing scores will scatter in a well known fashion. In an analysis
of variance one studies the way in which the scattering of scores departs from the
chance pattern.

In such an analysis one considers, for example, the three following: (1) the score

At the same time we recognize that some students of statistical analysis may have technical misgivings about the use of this method. Indeed, the literature of parapsychology shows that a substantial group of practicing scientists will be found to have objections to any one method of treating ESP data.

It seemed to us that it might be reassuring to the statistician and also to the layman to take some representative portion of our data and to examine it by various tests in addition to the analysis of variance. For this purpose we have chosen the seven series of individually tested subjects listed in Table 3. The sheep-goat effect here is stronger on the average than in the later group tests, so that any statistical misbehavior might reasonably be expected to become evident; at the same time the task of multiple analysis of this limited number of data is still within manageable proportions.

The analysis of variance of the data of Table 3 is given in Table 4. The unit of analysis which was adopted in this and all similar later tables of the book is the number of successes in 25 card guesses. The distribution of such "run scores" is binomial under the chance hypothesis. While it might be obvious to some readers that, with the parameters and numbers of the data here involved, the binomial model approximates the constant-variance normal adequately enough to allow an analysis of variance upon the raw scores, others might draw confidence from an empirical test of the matter. It will be seen in Table 4 that the variance and tests of

---

obtained for each run of 25 cards, (2) the total score for each subject, (3) the total score for all sheep, etc. The scatter of the run scores obtained by the first subject, combined with all the corresponding scatters of the other subjects, gives the "within-subject variance." Similarly, the scatter of the subject total scores of a group of subjects gives the "among-subject variance" for that group. And in the same way, one may find the variance between the sheep total and the goat total.

By comparing such variances, one with another, the experimenter can test various hypotheses about the data. The hypotheses are usually tested by the "null method." One asks, "If such and such an effect does not exist, how frequently (in numerous hypothetical repetitions of the experiment) would I get by chance alone so large an apparent effect as the one I actually observed?" If the answer is "very seldom" (i.e. if the probability is small), one may then choose to conclude that the observed score did not occur simply by chance and that either the effect was real or the experimental procedure was defective.

If one is comparing only two groups, such as sheep and goats, the *scatter* reduces to a *difference* and the usual analysis of variance test reduces to a simpler test, known as a "*t*-test."

TABLE 4. ANALYSIS OF VARIANCE OF ESP SCORES AMONG SUBJECTS WHO WERE TESTED INDIVIDUALLY BY SCHMEIDLER
(Data of Table 3)

SOURCE OF VARIATION	DEGREES OF FREEDOM	RAW SCORE VARIANCE	ARC SINE VARIANCE †
Binominal theory	inf.	4.00	4.00 ‡
Within sheep	944	4.19	3.99
Within goats	813	3.89	4.00
Among sheep	104	3.49	3.31
Among goats	33	4.69	4.61
Among series	12	4.23	4.13
Among subjects §	149	3.82	3.66
Sheep vs. goats	1	63.0	62.0
Sheep vs. theory	(1)	55.5	54.4
Goats vs. theory	(1)	15.8	15.7

EXCEPT AS FOLLOWS, NONE OF THE ABOVE VALUES REACH THE P = 0.05 LEVEL OF SIGNIFICANCE

	F	DEGREES OF FREEDOM	t	P
Sheep vs. goats:				
Raw score	$\dfrac{63.0}{3.82} = 16.5$	$\binom{1}{149}$	4.06	0.000,08
Arc sine	$\dfrac{62.0}{3.66} = 16.9$		4.11	0.000,06
Sheep vs. theory:				
Raw score	$\dfrac{55.5}{4.00} = 13.9$	$\binom{1}{\text{inf.}}$	3.73	0.000,19
Arc sine	$\dfrac{54.4}{4.00} = 13.6$		3.69	0.000,22
Goats vs. theory:				
Raw score	$\dfrac{15.8}{4.00} = 3.95$	$\binom{1}{\text{inf.}}$	1.99	0.047
Arc sine	$\dfrac{15.7}{4.00} = 3.92$		1.98	0.048

† *Converted score = arc sin $\sqrt{raw\ percentage\ score}$.*
‡ *The variance of the transformation of the actual model, normalized to this value.*
§ *Ignoring series.*

significance have been computed both for the actual number of successful card guesses and for an arc-sine transformation of the number of guesses [Kendall, 1951, 2, 206]. The differences in all cases are found to be unimportant. A further discussion is given in Appendix B.

In Table 4 the variances, within subjects, among subjects, and among series, are all within the limits of reasonable chance fluctuation. The variance between sheep and goats, on the other hand, is highly significant, with a *t* of 4.11 and 149 degrees of freedom. One concludes that the mean score of the sheep population is different from the mean score of the goat. Moreover, the total score of the sheep differs significantly from the binomial chance model (P = .0002), and the goat score likewise (P = .05).

Although there are no theoretical or internal empirical reasons for doubting that these data do meet the normality requirements for an analysis of variance, independent evidence for the reality of the sheep-goat influence upon ESP scoring can be obtained by

TABLE 5. INDEPENDENCE OF ATTRIBUTES AMONG SHEEP AND GOATS WHO WERE TESTED INDIVIDUALLY FOR ESP BY SCHMEIDLER
(Data of Table 3)

	ESP SCORES RELATIVE TO CHANCE EXPECTATION			TOTAL
	Above	*At*	*Below*	
Sheep:				
Observed	67	10	34	—
Adjusted	72	—	39	111
Expected	62.85	—	48.15	—
Deviation	+9.15	—	−9.15	—
Goats:				
Observed	13	1	26	—
Adjusted	13.5	—	26.5	40
Expected	22.65	—	17.35	—
Deviation	−9.15	—	+9.15	—
Total	85.5	—	65.5	151

$\chi^2 = 10.36$, *d.f.* = 1; *or* t = 3.22, *d.f.* = *inf.*
P = 0.0013, *with Yates' correction.*

applying an interaction test to a two-by-two table in which sheep and goats are divided according to whether they scored above or below the level of chance expectation. As shown in Table 5, the null hypothesis then yields a probability less than .002.

The understanding of the nature of ESP may ultimately be assisted by detailed study of how ESP data depart from the chance binomial model. Table 6 presents a goodness-of-fit test applied to the run scores of sheep and goats, separately and in combination. This test is less sensitive than the analysis of variance to a simple shifting of mean score (binomial p), but more sensitive to some other possible kinds of departure from a theoretical model.

It was found that for the goats separately and for sheep and goats combined, the run score distribution is not significantly different from the theoretical model with p equal to one-fifth. For sheep alone, however, the chance probability of the observed distribution is .001.

The question naturally arises as to whether this large goodness-of-fit chi-square reflects anything more than a shifting of the mean score, which was already shown to have a chance probability of .0002. Inspection of the individual deviations of the distribution of run scores from the theoretical model does not answer this question. However, a recomputation of goodness-of-fit using a model with the empirical p-value, yields a chi-square, significant at the .05 probability level. This suggests that, as one might in general expect, the ESP effect cannot be represented as a simple shift in the probability of guessing correctly in a single trial. Possibly ESP manifests itself in spurts lasting over several trials. However, the ESP effect both here and in the later group tests, would seem to be too weak to allow a test of this speculation. Nor, it might be remarked, are the data of Table 3 suitable to allow a goodness-of-fit test upon the total scores of the individual subjects.

What further tests can be applied to the observed distribution of run scores? The analysis of variance has already tested the first and second moments, and this examination has been extended in Table 7. The skewness of the sheep exceeds one standard deviation, but is intermediate between the binomial and the normal. The kurtosis of the sheep departs from the binomial by 1.5 standard deviations and from the normal curve by still less. Its negative

TABLE 6. BINOMIAL GOODNESS-OF-FIT OF ESP RUN SCORES. SUBJECTS TESTED INDIVIDUALLY BY SCHMEIDLER
(Data of Table 3)

	RUN SCORE (for 25 guesses)										χ^2	d.f.	P
	0+1	2	3	4	5	6	7	8	9	10+			
MODEL $p = 0.20000$													
Sheep (1055 runs):													
Observed	23.	69.	134.	161.	203.	195.	119.	89.	46.	16.	27.7	9	0.0011
Deviation	−5.9	−5.7	−9.3	−35.9	−3.8	+22.6	+2.1	+23.3	+15.0	−2.4			
Goats (853 runs):													
Observed	28.	62.	124.	175.	165.	127.	88.	48.	23.	13.	5.5	9	0.8
Deviation	+4.6	+1.6	+8.2	+15.7	−2.2	−12.4	−6.5	− 5.1	− 2.1	−1.8			
All subjects:													
Observed	51.	131.	258.	336.	368.	322.	207.	137.	69.	29.	8.1	9	0.5
Deviation	−1.3	−4.1	−1.1	−20.2	−6.0	+10.2	−4.4	+18.2	+12.9	−4.2			
MODEL $p = 0.20410$													
Sheep (1055 runs):													
Observed	23.	69.	134.	161.	203.	195.	119.	89.	46.	16.	17.2	9	0.046
Deviation	−3.0	−0.1	−1.9	−30.8	−3.5	+18.5	−3.9	+18.1	+11.6	−5.0			

value indicates a slightly flattened distribution with a deficit of extreme scores.

It has already been shown that with these data the application of the arc-sine transformation is a needless refinement in the analysis of variance. The statistical constants now reveal that the

TABLE 7. STATISTICAL CONSTANTS OF RUN SCORES OF SUBJECTS WHO WERE TESTED INDIVIDUALLY BY SCHMEIDLER
(Data of Table 3)

	MEAN $\mu_1' = \kappa_1$	VARIANCE $\mu_2 = \kappa_2$	SKEWNESS $\sqrt{\beta_1} = \dfrac{\kappa_3}{\kappa_2^{3/2}}$	KURTOSIS $\beta_2 - 3 = \dfrac{\kappa_4}{\kappa_2^{2}}$
Normal	5.000	4.000	0	0
Binomial	5.000	4.000	+0.3000	+0.0100
Sheep:				
Observed	5.2294	4.1067	+0.1808	−0.2121
σ	0.06157	0.1747	0.0753 †	0.1505 †
C.R.‡	3.73	0.61	1.58	1.48
Goats:				
Observed	4.8640	3.9415	+0.3323	−0.0680
σ	0.06848	0.1943	0.0837 †	0.1672 †
C.R.‡	1.99	0.30	0.39	0.47

† *Under the normal hypothesis.*
‡ *Of difference between observed statistic and theoretical binomial parameter.*

run-score distributions approximate the binomial model quite closely. Moreover, there would seem to be no basis for rejecting for reasons of non-normality the application of the analysis of variance to the raw scores of the group-gathered data of the following chapter. There the accordance with the chance binomial model is, on the whole, even closer than for the present individually gathered data.

Summary

After 151 subjects had been individually tested in a total of 47,700 card-guessing trials, the mean score of the "sheep" population was found higher than that of the "goat" at the .000,06 level of significance. Moreover, the total sheep score departed from the chance model with a significant probability of .0002, and the goat score departed (in the opposite direction) with a suggestive probability of .05. The applicability of the analysis of variance to the raw run scores of these subjects and the significance of the sheep-goat separation were tested by an arc-sine transformation, a chi-square test for independence of attributes among subjects, goodness-of-fit tests to the binomial distribution, and the computation and evaluation of the higher moments of the observed distributions.

CHAPTER 5

Group Tests of Sheep and Goats

In 1945 the classroom administration of ESP tests was begun with the hope of increasing research productivity. This work overlapped the last of the individual series and continued through the spring of 1951. The major part of the book is based upon the data of this period.

In the group testing, as in the individual tests already described, basic experimental safeguards were maintained: subjects had no normal method of observing or inferring the target order, the experimenter gave no clues as to this order, and the subjects were asked to designate themselves as sheep or goats before they knew their ESP scores.[1] However, the group sessions naturally differed in many respects from the sessions where a single subject was tested, and minor changes were introduced from one group session to the next. Some classes had been told about the general nature of the research and were, for the most part, eager to act as subjects; others were unprepared. The experimental room was sometimes uncomfortably stuffy. It was sometimes so large that it was difficult to hear the instructions. Some subjects were hurried (and in a few cases did not complete the assigned number of responses), whereas some who worked quickly had tedious delays. Some were permitted to check the results of the earlier runs before they made the later ones; others were not told their scores. It seems useless to itemize these and other similar minor differences for each of the 37 separate classroom administrations, for when so many conditions are casually or accidentally varied in the absence of a previously determined experimental design, it is unlikely that any can be sufficiently isolated for study. We shall therefore limit ourselves to describing one typical group session in some detail, and shall also discuss one condition that all the group administrations

1. See, however, Appendix B, p. 125.

had in common: the fact that all members of a single class guessed at the same target lists.

Before this typical session the subjects had been told a little about the experiment and about psychic research. Perhaps the few absentees represented the students most hostile to ESP research or least interested in experimentation, but no attempt was made to check on this possibility. As they came into the room each subject was given two stapled sets of papers. One consisted of two identical pages, with carbon paper between. On the pages were mimeographed nine columns of twenty-five squares each. The top sheet and the carbon paper were cut between the third and fourth columns, and also between the sixth and seventh. Above the second, fifth and eighth columns a number was written which identified the subject. The other set of papers consisted of a blank sheet and another half-size sheet, numbered to correspond with the first set. On the half-sheet there was space for a name and the incomplete sentence, "I am a $\frac{sheep}{goat}$ because . . ." Below was mimeographed a three-inch horizontal line with the ends and center marked by short vertical slashes. At the left was written "Belief that guesses of this kind can be successful"; at the right was written "Complete disbelief."

The class was told that lists had been prepared which were made up of five symbols. (If they inquired about the location of the lists, they were shown a glimpse of the sealed, opaque envelopes, on the instructor's desk, which contained the lists.) [2] Sample ESP cards representing these symbols were put in front of the class, leaning on the blackboard, where they remained for the rest of the period. The class was told, further, that the symbols

2. In certain cases this concealed-target procedure was modified to permit the possible operation of telepathy as well as clairvoyance. In the modified procedure the target symbols were looked at one at a time by a student or by the instructor while the class made their responses. When a student was to act as the "sender," he carried sealed targets and a synchronized timer into an adjacent room. When the instructor looked at the targets, she did so without speaking and with the targets screened from the class. She did not wear eyeglasses (which in theory might reflect the target image). Less than 9 per cent of the data of Table 8 were gathered in this way and no significant difference was found between these and the remaining data. For the sheep, the observed-target and concealed-target run-score averages were 5.17 and 5.10 respectively. For the goats, the corresponding averages were 4.98 and 4.92. Data gathered in this exceptional fashion have been listed with the American Documentation Institute (see below, p. 123).

had been arranged in random order, and thus might appear in any sequence; and that each symbol on a list might appear any number of times, from zero to twenty-five. Their task was to guess the order of symbols on the list, indicating that order by filling in the appropriate boxes on the sheets before them. They were to indicate the symbols by certain short-cuts (*W* for wavy lines, *S* for star, etc.), and the marks they were to use were written on the blackboard, each above the appropriate card. Before they made their responses, they were to write their names on the half-sheet of paper before them. The distinction between "sheep" and "goat" was explained. They were instructed to cross out the inappropriate word, and to give the reason for their choice by completing the sentence and adding others if necessary. They were then to indicate, on the line below, their position on the continuum extending from belief that guesses in this task could be successful, to disbelief in it, using the midpoint of the line to show uncertainty. These instructions were repeated in condensed form for latecomers; questions from the class were answered; and the subjects were instructed to make their guesses for the first three lists, using pencil or ballpoint pen. Pencils were distributed to students who needed them.

When almost all the subjects had completed their responses for the first three runs, the others were asked to hurry. When all were done, they were instructed to tear off and hand in the strip of paper on which they had written. They retained the carbon copy of the responses. After the strips had been collected, the top opaque envelope was opened. The three target lists which it contained were read aloud, and the class was told to check correct responses. They were then told to draw a man on the sheet of blank paper before them. (Later cursory analysis revealed no obvious difference between drawings made by high scorers in ESP and by low scorers, and these data have not been reported.) While they were making the drawing, the experimenter fastened together and labeled the target lists and the material they had handed in. The class next filled in the fourth, fifth, and sixth columns on their record sheets, tore off and handed in the strips, and heard and checked the three corresponding target lists. Booklets for Rosenzweig's Picture-Frustration Study were distributed; the experimenter read the instructions; and the class filled out the booklets. While they were doing so, the experimenter fastened together and labeled the data for runs 4–6. On completing the booklets, the students made the last three ESP runs. The bell indicating the close of the period rang before these target lists could be read; the material was collected; and the session ended.

In reporting the above procedure, we do not recommend it to others. The formalized routine necessary in a class experiment, the pressure for speed on the slower subjects, and the long delays for the faster ones, all militate against the spontaneity that seems to help in ESP performance; and probably a session crammed as full as this one represents a particularly poor situation for eliciting ESP. There is also some evidence that three successive series of seventy-five uninterrupted ESP guesses will result in less interest (and in scores that are nearer chance expectation) than short series. Thus it now seems to us that this procedure, which accounts for most of the data here reported, is a poor one for testing ESP: it tends to obscure the very factors we are looking for and requires a large number of cases to delineate a trend which might have been shown more quickly if a better method had been used.

One technical difficulty that should be mentioned in a description of these group experiments is known as "multiple calling." This is the possibility of group preference for a certain target order. Suppose, for example, that most subjects make their first calls a "star." If they guess at the same list, and the list begins with a star, their "extra-chance" high scores are obviously not due to ESP. Nor, if the list does not begin with a star, are their "extra-chance" low scores due to ESP avoidance of the target. Although the danger of statistical error caused by multiple calling deserves serious consideration when subjects respond to only a few targets, it has been demonstrated that it may be dismissed when a great many target lists, each randomly determined, are used. The set of conditions under which it can be properly disregarded in group experiments has been the topic for both statistical and experimental research [Greville, 1944; Humphrey, 1949]. We shall refer the interested reader to Appendix B, page 122, and to Appendix C—which reports correspondence that analyzes the topic in more detail—and shall merely state for other readers that where upward of three hundred target lists are used, as in this research, the ordinary methods of evaluation can be employed with confidence.

In Table 8 are summarized the results for all sheep and all goats who have ever been tested by GRS in group experiments. The data are presented according to the academic semester in which the research was performed. Over all there is an unmistakable trend toward higher ESP scores for sheep than for goats. The difference between the two groups is statistically significant at the probability level of .ooo,o3. When the results of the group and individual experiments are combined, the resulting chance probability of the sheep-goat difference is about .ooo,ooo,1. However, it is also clear from Table 8 that the average difference in score between sheep and goats tested under group conditions is very small, and that the differences are variable. In only two out of 14 semesters did the sheep scores deviate significantly at the one per cent probability level from the chance expected value. There was not a single semester in which the goats had scores that were significantly different from the expected value. In two semesters the average score for goats was actually higher than for sheep. If individual classes had been listed, instead of grouping several classes together, more of these reversals would have been found.

The fact that these differences between average ESP scores of sheep and goats are so small and so variable might give rise to the question of whether they are authentic, or whether they are due only to small, cumulative, autistic errors in scoring, which finally have made the results conform to the experimenter's bias. So many precautions were taken to prevent autistic errors as to rule out the possibility of their being of any importance in the final results. To list briefly the major precautions:

1. In the original analysis each of the runs was given two independent scorings to ascertain the number of hits. These scorings were usually made by two different individuals. Whenever possible, and in every case where the two scorings were made by the same individual, one check was taken from the original records and the other from a carbon copy of them. It is therefore unlikely that many scoring errors remain undiscovered.

2. The total number of responses that were correct in each run was independently recorded in two separate places.

3. Group totals were computed and checked in the usual way. They were then subjected to many cross-checks, as further analyses were made of the data.

TABLE 8. ESP SCORES OF ALL SHEEP AND GOATS. SCHMEIDLER'S GROUP-ADMINISTERED EXPERIMENTS

ACADEMIC SEMESTER BEGINNING	SHEEP (accepting † ESP)				GOATS (rejecting † ESP)			
	Number of Sheep	Number of Runs (25 guesses)	Deviation from Chance Expectation	Mean Hits per Run ‡	Number of Goats	Number of Runs	Deviation from Chance Expectation	Mean Hits per Run ‡
Feb. '45	35	319	+ 52	5.16	38	344	− 63	4.82
Sept. '45	14	125	+ 43	5.34	7	65	+ 2	5.03
Feb. '46	80	712	+ 39	5.05	69	620	− 31	4.95
July '46	52	467	+ 39	5.08	81	729	−119	4.84
Sept. '46	37	333	− 22	4.93	9	81	− 3	4.96
Feb. '47	52	466	+ 69	5.15	53	477	+ 67	5.14
Sept. '47	56	504	+130	5.26	30	270	− 31	4.89
Feb. '48	63	505	+ 68	5.13	29	240	+ 15	5.06
Sept. '48	75	675	− 5	4.99	11	99	− 35	4.65
Feb. '49	63	567	+ 6	5.01	31	279	− 46	4.84
Sept. '49	52	468	− 8	4.98	20	180	− 53	4.71
Feb. '50	48	334	+ 47	5.14	26	194	+ 47	5.24
Sept. '50	37	294	+ 37	5.13	20	156	− 7	4.96
Feb. '51	28	216	+119	5.55	41	316	− 44	4.86
Total	692	5985	+614	5.10	465	4050	−301	4.93

† The possibility of ESP under the conditions of the experiment.
‡ Chance expected value is 5.00.

4. After November 1946 in most cases the ESP response sheets were identified only by a number. (An occasional student disobeyed instructions and wrote his name.) On a separate sheet that number was associated with the name of the subject, the designation of sheep or goat, and other identifying material. This precaution against autistic scoring errors is a perhaps unnecessary supplement to the procedure of paragraph 1 above, for it is unlikely that the same error would occur on independent scorings.

5. Whenever a subject's classification of himself as sheep or goat was unclear, he was categorized by the experimenter or a consultant without knowledge [3] of his ESP score.

6. While re-analyzing the data for presentation in this book, RAM has done an independent recheck from original documents of a representative sample of the data, as described in Appendix B.

So much for procedural precautions. What are the results in detail? The analysis of variance of the data of Table 8 is given in Table 9. (The nonmathematical reader may skip four pages to the end of this chapter.) The results follow closely the pattern found with the previous individually tested subjects. Using the pooled variance among subjects, we have tested the hypothesis that the sheep and goats are drawn from a common population. This hypothesis is evidently untenable (P = .000,03), as are likewise the suppositions that the sheep and goats separately are drawn from the theoretical binomial population for which p is one-fifth (P = .000,07 and .018, respectively).

In these group results there is one feature not found in the individual subject tests. If sheep and goat semesters are pooled, their variance is suggestively greater than the subject variance at the .03 probability level. This may be taken as a warning that there are important unknown (situational?) variables in testing for ESP— a fact well established by the research of others. It would be unwarranted, however, to assume that the semester variation is an adequate measure of all such variables.

Other variance comparisons might be made, but all of them fail to reach significance at the .05 probability level. Two such comparisons are shown in Table 9 because their nonsignificance is not obvious by inspection.

3. Knowledge, that is, by any normal means. No precautions were taken against the experimenter or consultant being guided by ESP.

TABLE 9. ANALYSIS OF VARIANCE OF ESP RUN SCORES.
ALL SHEEP AND GOATS IN SCHMEIDLER'S GROUP
EXPERIMENTS
(Data of Table 8)

SOURCE OF VARIATION	SUM OF SQUARES	DEGREES OF FREEDOM	VARIANCE
Binomial theory	—	inf.	4.000
Within sheep	21,326.	5,293	4.029
Within goats	13,966.	3,585	3.896
Among sheep	2,844.	678	4.195
Among goats	1,925.	451	4.268
Sheep semesters	97.2	13	7.48
Goat semesters	77.6	13	5.97
Sheep vs. goats	75.6	1	75.6
Sheep vs. theory	—	(1)	63.0
Goats vs. theory	—	(1)	22.4
Total	40,311.4	10,034	—

SOURCE OF VARIATION	F	DEGREES OF FREEDOM	C.R. OR t	P
Within sheep vs. within goats	$\dfrac{4.029}{3.896}$	$\left(\dfrac{5293}{3585}\right)$	1.09	0.28
Among subjects vs. within subjects	$\dfrac{4.224}{3.975}$	$\left(\dfrac{1129}{8878}\right)$	1.38	0.08
Among semesters	$\dfrac{6.72}{4.224}$	$\left(\dfrac{26}{1129}\right)$	—	~0.03
Sheep vs. goats	$\dfrac{75.6}{4.281}$	$\left(\dfrac{1}{1155}\right)$	4.20	0.000,03
Sheep vs. theory	$\dfrac{63.0}{4.000}$	$\left(\dfrac{1}{\text{inf.}}\right)$	3.97	0.000,07
Goats vs. theory	$\dfrac{22.4}{4.000}$	$\left(\dfrac{1}{\text{inf.}}\right)$	2.37	0.018

In the case of the individual subjects a goodness-of-fit test of
run scores showed with suggestive significance that ESP could
not be represented by a simple shift of Bernoullian trial probability. Similar tests for run scores and subject scores are given in
Tables 10 and 11 for the group-gathered data of Table 8. All the
distributions are marginally significant when tested against the
theoretical binomial model for a p of one-fifth, but it is obvious

TABLE 10. BINOMIAL GOODNESS-OF-FIT OF ESP RUN SCORES. ALL SUBJECTS WHO WERE TESTED IN GROUPS BY SCHMEIDLER
(Data of Table 8)

	RUN SCORE (for 25 guesses)										χ^2	d.f.	P
	0 + 1	2	3	4	5	6	7	8	9	10+			
Sheep (5985 runs):													
Observed	146.	394.	760.	1123.	1134.	1008.	704.	405.	193.	118.			
Deviation †	−17.9	−30.0	−52.6	+ 5.7	−39.1	+30.4	+40.6	+31.8	+16.8	+14.3	18.5	9	0.030
Goats (4050 runs):													
Observed	126.	289.	556.	787.	797.	690.	397.	225.	126.	57.			
Deviation †	+15.1	+ 2.1	+ 6.1	+30.9	+ 3.2	+28.4	−51.9	−27.5	+ 6.8	−13.2	16.5	9	0.057

† *From binomial model with $p = 1/5$.*

TABLE 11. BINOMIAL GOODNESS-OF-FIT OF ESP TOTAL SCORES. SUBJECTS WHO WERE TESTED IN GROUPS BY SCHMEIDLER
(All Subjects from Table 8 Who Did 8 or 9 Runs)

EIGHT-RUN SUBJECTS (200 guesses)	0–35	36–38	39–41	42–44	45+	χ^2	d.f.	P
109 Sheep								
Observed	15.	14.	23.	22.	35.			
Deviation †	−8.4	− 6.4	+0.2	+2.6	+12.0	11.6	4	0.021
81 Goats								
Observed	22.	5.	20.	13.	21.			
Deviation †	+4.6	−10.2	+3.1	−1.4	+ 3.9	9.7	4	0.046

NINE-RUN SUBJECTS (225 guesses)	0–34	35–36	37–38	39–40	41–42	43–44	45–46	47–48	49–50	51–52	53–54	55–56	57+	χ^2	d.f.	P
526 Sheep																
Observed	9.	24.	32.	49.	53.	67.	68.	55.	47.	40.	34.	28.	20.			
Deviation †	−10.3	+3.6	−1.1	+1.5	−7.4	−1.3	− 1.0	−7.7	−4.2	+2.3	+8.8	+12.7	+4.1	23.3	12	0.025
363 Goats																
Observed	18.	22.	30.	30.	45.	52.	28.	50.	30.	25.	16.	9.	8.			
Deviation †	+ 4.7	+7.9	+7.1	−2.8	+3.3	+4.9	−19.7	+6.8	−5.3	−1.0	−1.4	− 1.5	−3.0	20.5	12	0.058

† From binomial model with $p = 1/5$.

by inspection of the distribution deviations that these scores would conform in an uninteresting fashion to models with empirical trial probabilities. Thus this finding in the individual data is not sustained in the group data. Since nonbinomiality is probably a characteristic of psi trials, its apparent absence here might be due to the weakness of the ESP.

Summary

A total of 250,875 ESP card trials made by 1157 subjects in classroom groups confirmed the previous finding that those who accepted the possibility of paranormal success under the conditions of the experiment would score higher than those who did not ($P = .000,03$), and that both the accepting "sheep" and the rejecting "goats" would exhibit mean scores departing significantly from the chance binomial model ($P = .000,07$ and $.02$ respectively).

CHAPTER 6

ESP Acceptance: A Survey

FROM the foregoing research there seems to be no doubt that, in the populations studied, answers to the sheep-goat question separate two groups that give significant differences in ESP scores. Presumably the answers reflect differences in attitude, but we have still to find what those differences are. In itself, the sheep-goat dichotomy is not very revealing. We begin with a large group of subjects, most of whom have never considered seriously the question of paranormal perception; we outline an arbitrary experimental procedure in which they are to take part; and then we ask them for a clear-cut opinion about it. Social pressure forces them to choose between two categories, and a forced choice between alternatives that are familiar to some subjects but unfamiliar to others must result in heterogeneous groups.

It seems necessary to expand on this point, even though it is repetitious; for unless the subgroups among sheep and goats are analyzed and found to be similar, it cannot be expected that two separate experiments, which put the sheep-goat question to different populations, should give similar results. Some sheep, for example, are convinced that they can score well; some think that it may be possible for others to have paranormal success under these conditions, but that they themselves are not likely to do so; some will say that they don't know, that they want to wait and see what happens; still others that they think it is probably only a matter of chance as to whether or not they will succeed but they are not sure—perhaps there is some possibility of ESP. Among the goats there are (to cite only a few examples) those who dismiss the whole procedure as laughable and never give it serious consideration; others who have thought about the problem and calmly decided that ESP is an impossibility; some who indignantly and vehemently protest against the absurdity of ESP research; and still others who express deep interest in and sympathy for the possibility of telepathy but consider that the impersonal design of this procedure, which their stubborn experimenter has foolishly imposed, will make paranormal success impossible under *these* conditions.

In addition to the variety of intellectual attitudes, there are some sheep who approach the problem with boredom, others with a hope that they can score well, others with a fear of the unknown that this topic evokes. Some goats will enjoy the procedure because it is like a game, some will resent it as a waste of time, and some will feel guilty because of their rejection of the basic plan of the experiment and try particularly hard to cooperate in the guessing so as to make amends. It must be clear that this list of possibilities could be extended further, and that whatever meaning lies in the sheep-goat dichotomy can be understood only when such aspects of it are taken into consideration.

One step in the direction of such consideration has been taken by several experimenters in certain studies of the acceptance or rejection of the possibility of paranormal success which divide the data into more than two levels. In most cases the subjects whose attitudes were most favorable to ESP had higher ESP scores than the subjects whose attitudes were least favorable to ESP. There were, however, exceptions and also so many variations in the details of the findings that it is obvious that more research is needed before we can understand the dynamics of what occurred. And without understanding the dynamics, we do not know what conditions need to be controlled to obtain consistent results. Perhaps it was only a series of coincidences that subjects in different situations with different experimenters gave results which were even roughly consistent with one another and with our results—but probably it is better scientific method to assume, tentatively, that it was something more than coincidence. We shall discuss the problem at greater length after the various experiments have been reported.

The first of these studies, by Bevan [1947], made four divisions of attitude. On the basis of discussion following the question "Do you accept ESP as an established fact?" the subjects were divided into three groups: emphatically positive, indecisive, and emphatically negative. Bevan then described the procedure, and asked, "Do you think ESP can be measured by the techniques (which have just been explained)?" Subjects who were either emphatically positive or indecisive in answering the first question, but gave a negative answer to the second question, were transferred to a fourth group, "mixed." This group was disqualified by Bevan from acting as subjects.

In the series where subjects were required to respond to ESP cards, Bevan's results showed an over-all trend similar to that of our subjects, but with somewhat higher average scores (Table 12). Subjects who gave an emphatically positive answer scored sugges-

TABLE 12. BEVAN'S DATA ON ESP SCORES RELATED TO ATTITUDE GROUPS

ATTITUDE TOWARD THE POSSIBILITY OF ESP UNDER THE CONDITIONS OF THE EXPERIMENT	NUMBER OF SUBJECTS	NUMBER OF RUNS (*25 guesses*)	DEVIATION FROM CHANCE EXPECTATION	MEAN HITS PER RUN †
Emphatically positive	10	116	+44	5.38
Indecisive	10	116	+66	5.57
Emphatically negative	10	120	+ 2	5.02

† *Chance expected value is 5.00.*

tively above chance; subjects who gave an indecisive answer scored above chance at the significance level of .002, and these two groups, pooled to permit direct comparison with our subjects (since both correspond to our sheep), had an average ESP score higher than those who gave an emphatically negative answer, with a difference probability of about .04.

Woodruff and Dale [1950] as a part of a broader investigation sought correlations between ESP card scores and the subject's belief in ESP and estimate of his own ESP ability. The data, based upon 49 subjects, were not presented in detail in the original paper, but a high-low grouping of favorableness to ESP showed no significant differences.

Asking his subjects whether they believed in ESP, Casper [1951] divided them into three groups, which will be called here the believers, indecisives, and disbelievers. He does not seem to have inquired as to whether his subjects believed that ESP could function in the test situation. It is therefore possible that some of his "believers" and "indecisives" belong among our goats. Casper's data are shown in Table 13. The believers scored higher at ESP than the disbelievers; the indecisives had the lowest scores, unlike Bevan's indecisives. (Since the key questions were slightly different, and especially since Bevan rated his subjects' attitudes after discus-

TABLE 13. CASPER'S DATA ON ESP SCORES RELATED TO ATTITUDE GROUPS

SUBJECTS' ATTITUDES	NUMBER OF SUBJECTS	NUMBER OF RUNS (25 guesses)	DEVIATION FROM CHANCE EXPECTATION	MEAN HITS PER RUN
Believe in ESP	81	324	+51	5.16
Indecisive	52	208	−63	4.70
Disbelieve in ESP	13	52	− 8	4.85

sion, while Casper in one of his series used written answers on a short questionnaire, Bevan's and Casper's "indecisives" may represent somewhat different groups.) For Casper, the difference between believers on the one hand and indecisives plus disbelievers on the other, is significant at about the .01 probability level, without correction for selection of the analysis.

A similar analysis was made by Kahn [1952] as a minor part of a rigorously controlled ESP experiment which, over all, showed significantly positive results. In two of his five series, subjects filled out a questionnaire relating to their attitudes toward ESP success (Table 14). It will be noted that those of Kahn's subjects who consider that ESP is impossible here but possible elsewhere would, according to Bevan's procedure, have been called "mixed" and would not have been tested. According to our procedure, they would have been grouped among the goats. None of Kahn's deviations is statistically significant, and by our definitions his sheep-goat difference is close to zero.

Somewhat earlier, Eilbert [Eilbert and Schmeidler, 1950] investigated the problem of belief in ESP, in the course of an experiment on ESP responses while the subject was listening to different musical selections. After describing the procedure, he inquired about the subject's attitude, and classified each person as either (a) believing in ESP and thinking he will do well in this experiment, (b) believing in ESP but doubting that he will do well in this experiment, (c) doubtful about the whole subject, (d) rejecting ESP completely, or (e) giving irrelevant or contradictory answers. His results are listed in Table 15. It will be noted that the break-off point in his data comes between the subjects who believe in ESP (groups a and b) and those who are doubtful about it or reject it (groups c and d). The difference between the pooled ESP scores of groups a and b and the pooled ESP scores of groups c and d is suggestive at about the .04 probability level, without correction for selection.

TABLE 14. KAHN'S DATA ON ESP SCORES RELATED TO SUBJECTS' STATEMENTS OF BELIEF IN THE POSSIBILITY OF ESP

SUBJECTS' STATEMENTS	NUMBER OF SUBJECTS	NUMBER OF RUNS (*25 guesses*)	DEVIATION FROM CHANCE EXPECTATION	MEAN HITS PER RUN
ESP is possible here and elsewhere	62	733.20	+42.0	5.06
ESP is impossible here but possible elsewhere	8	95.48	+21.6	5.23
ESP is impossible anywhere	4	47.88	− 9.4	4.80

The data from GRS's subjects do not throw any further light on the question of where a division between favorable and unfavorable attitudes should be made. During the seven semesters after GRS had seen Bevan's and Eilbert's data, she attempted (before seeing the ESP scores) to divide subjects into four groups: sheep(+), who seemed to think it possible to attain paranormal success under the conditions of the experiment; sheep(?), who were doubtful about it; sheep(−), who considered it unlikely; and goats, who considered it impossible. Since, during these years, all her subjects were tested in classroom experiments, no sensitive clinical determinations could be made. Subjects were assigned to the different groups either by themselves, or on the basis of comments they made both to the uncompleted sentence, "I am a sheep/goat" be-

TABLE 15. EILBERT'S DATA ON ESP SCORES RELATED TO ATTITUDE GROUPS

SUBJECTS' ATTITUDES	NUMBER OF SUBJECTS	NUMBER OF RUNS (*25 guesses*)	DEVIATION FROM CHANCE EXPECTATION	MEAN HITS PER RUN
a. Believe in ESP and think they will do well in this experiment	3	15	+ 8	5.53
b. Believe in ESP but doubt they will do well in this experiment	11	55	+33	5.60
c. Doubtful about the whole topic	23	115	− 2	4.98
d. Reject ESP completely	4	20	− 2	4.90
e. Give irrelevant or contradictory answers	9	45	− 2	4.96

cause . . ." and to certain other incomplete sentences, mentioned further in Chapter 9. Table 16 summarizes the results. It shows negligible differences among the three classes of sheep, but a significant difference between the sheep (taken as a whole) and the goats.

TABLE 16. SCHMEIDLER'S SUBDIVISION OF SHEEP ATTITUDES
(Data Gathered February 1948 to May 1951)

SUBJECTS' ATTITUDES	NUMBER OF SUBJECTS	NUMBER OF RUNS (*25 guesses*)	DEVIATION FROM CHANCE EXPECTATION	MEAN HITS PER RUN
Sheep(+): think it probable that there can be ESP under these conditions	61	519	+ 46	5.09
Sheep(?): undecided	175	1426	+ 88	5.06
Sheep(−): think it unlikely that there should be ESP under these conditions	121	1034	+114	5.11
Goats: think it impossible that there should be ESP under these conditions	163	1329	−128	4.90

A recent study relating to the sheep-goat question is that by Smith and Canon [1954]. These experimenters used a left-right choice as the ESP target ($p = \frac{1}{2}$); but, unknown to the subjects, they made up only two lists of targets, the one consisting entirely of "lefts" and the other consisting entirely of "rights." They divided their subjects according to the question "Do you think that ESP ever actually occurs?" (Presumably some of the "believers" would be classified as goats if the dichotomizing question had referred to belief in the occurrence of ESP *within the test situation*.) Subjects were instructed in the classroom but made their responses at home.

Making allowance for the expected lefthand bias, the experimenters found that the 372 believers scored at a rate above the 88 nonbelievers, with a difference of 1.52 in the success-per-trial percentages. Although this difference in scoring rate is about what we observed in individual sessions (1.48 per cent) and well above what we found in group tests (.68 per cent), their results fail to reach statistical significance with the relatively small number of data (25 guesses per subject).

TABLE 17. VAN DE CASTLE'S DATA† ON ESP SCORES RELATED TO ATTITUDE GROUPS

SUBJECT'S ATTITUDE TOWARD ESP	NUMBER OF SUBJECTS	NUMBER OF RUNS (*25 guesses*)	DEVIATION FROM CHANCE EXPECTATION	MEAN HITS PER RUN
Positive	141	1004	+80	5.08
Conflict	61	536	+10	5.02
Negative	96	636	−35	4.94

† *Data gathered by Van de Castle, alone and jointly with others, published and unpublished.*

In a continuing study in connection with other problems, Van de Castle has divided subjects according to their acceptance of the reality of ESP. Table 17 is a condensation of his data, some of them published [Van de Castle and White, 1955], showing three attitude categories: positive, negative, and conflict. The positive group scored above chance expectation and the negative below, but the difference is not statistically significant.

Here, then, are six or seven out of eight investigators, with re-

sults showing a general trend toward higher ESP scores for subjects who accorded some measure of acceptance to the ESP hypothesis than for subjects who rejected it, but with differences in the
detailed findings.[1] There are many possible explanations for these
differences. Most of the deviations were comparatively small, and
in those cases the data may represent random fluctuations. Some
of the categories, though they seem precise logically, may be vague
psychologically; probably, for example, Eilbert's qualitative descriptions are better than our more quantitative ones. Statements
made by subjects in response to a questionnaire may be less meaningful than statements made by a careful experimenter after he
has listened to his subjects and observed them, either because the
subjects use different frames of reference for evaluating their own
doubt or acceptance, while the experimenter's standard of reference is uniform, or perhaps because on this curious topic the subjects are not fully aware of their own attitudes. We shall suggest
a further kind of explanation, which we believe to be important.

It is obvious that the experimenter, by his personality and
presentation, may affect the subject's self-classification as a sheep
or goat. Not so obvious is the possibility that the experimenter
may directly influence the ESP performance—even to the extent
of unwittingly suppressing the sought-for phenomenon. That this
could happen was established by Pratt and Price [1938] in a col-
laborative investigation growing out of the anomalous discovery
that, with similar groups of orphanage children, Price had obtained highly significant results and Pratt only chance results. The
same sort of thing may have occurred among the investigators who
sought for a sheep-goat effect. What possible psychological mechanisms could account for this kind of suppression of ESP?

1. For completeness' sake we mention a related study. Grela [1945] selected 11
subjects on the basis of their positive response to the sway test of suggestibility.
Each subject made three series of ESP card tests. The first was a control series without direct suggestion. For a total of 95 card decks the average number of correct
guesses was 5.40. In the second series the subject was hypnotized, told that he would
be card-tested upon awaking, and that he knew that telepathy was possible and
that he would succeed with it. There were 79 runs averaging 5.62. In the third
series the subject was rehypnotized and told he would be card-tested but that he
was convinced that he possessed no ESP ability and that ESP did not exist. In this
series there were 70 runs with a mean score of 5.29. The differences among the series
are not statistically significant although the chance probability of the combined
scores is .0006.

The pressure upon the subject may have been different with different experimenters, and may have varied also between the individual and the group sessions. In an individual experiment, with an experimenter who is clearly sympathetic to ESP and who has a likable personality, the subject who expresses the same sympathy may feel a rapport and an acceptance which permits a freer response, and thus a higher number of ESP successes, than would otherwise appear. A carefully noncommittal experimenter, or one whom the subject dislikes, or one who puts pressure on the subject to succeed, may elicit a very different mood in the subject who has already declared himself as unreservedly in favor of the ESP hypothesis. In the classroom, moreover, the subject who is more sympathetic to ESP than most of the rest of the class may react to the knowledge that he is "different" by becoming constrained, awkward, and defensive; this reaction may bring down his ESP scores. The classroom subjects who held the more popular attitudes—in Table 16, the sheep(?) and the sheep(—)—might feel more confident and at ease.

All of these hypotheses are susceptible to experimental test. It would be interesting to check on them, always taking into account, of course, the attitude of the experimenter, since he is an important member of either the individual session or the classroom group.

Consideration of the variability of motive patterns in relation to the experiment led us to try another approach. For many subjects, the question of the possibility of paranormal success is difficult, unfamiliar, and unduly abstract. They are neither much interested in it nor very consistent in their response to it, and thus we should not expect a clear relationship between their response to it and their ESP guesses. We should, however, expect to find such a relationship among subjects to whom such theoretical problems are important and who like to guide their behavior in terms of being theoretically consistent. A test which essays to measure this trait is the Allport-Vernon Study of Values [1931], which rates subjects according to the relative importance, for them, of Spranger's six values: theoretical, economic, aesthetic, social, political and religious. The definitions of these terms as they are used in the Allport-Vernon Study are different from common usage, but the first is particularly apt for our purposes. The individual with a high rating for theoretical values is described as having as his dominant interest the discovery of truth.

Following this line of reasoning, which was based on observation of our subjects, we suggested [Schmeidler, 1950a] that only when high theoretical scores were obtained on the Allport-Vernon Study of Values should the sheep-goat dichotomy be expected to discriminate efficiently between high-scoring ESP subjects and low-scoring ones. Subsequent subjects were accordingly given the Values Study to fill out, as well as the sheep-goat question.

TABLE 18. "THEORY INTEREST" AND ACCEPTANCE OF ESP
(Schmeidler's Data Taken with the Allport-Vernon *Study of Values*)

THEORY INTEREST (Percentile rank, college norms)	SHEEP		GOATS	
	Number of Subjects (200 guesses each)	Mean Score (25 guesses)	Number of Subjects	Mean Score
0–60	29	5.15	28	4.95
60–80	16	5.26	15	4.90
80–100	15	5.68	11	4.85
0–100	60	5.31	54	4.92

ANALYSIS OF VARIANCE BY THE METHOD OF UNWEIGHTED MEANS
(*Division of Theory Interest at the 60th Percentile*)

CATEGORY	d.f.	VARIANCE (25 guesses)	F	t	P
Binomial theory	inf.	4.00	—	—	—
Within subjects	798	3.89	—	—	—
Among subjects	110	4.85	—	—	—
Sheep vs. goats	1	34.90	34.90/4.85	2.68 †	0.010
Theory interest	1	3.32	—	—	—
Interaction	1	8.37	8.37/4.85	1.31	0.20

† *The method of harmonically weighted differences yields the same value.*

The data from 114 subjects are presented in Table 18. Eight other subjects who completed less than the standard number of 200 guesses were omitted to facilitate analysis after it was determined that their distribution and scores could have no appreciable influence on the results. The 50th percentile of "theory interest" in this sample of City College students fell at the 60th percentile of the Allport-Vernon college norms. Consequently we have divided the subjects at that point for the analysis of variance. The sheep-goat difference is significant, as expected. The calculation of importance is the "interaction," which tells whether the sheep-goat effect depends upon interest in theory. The resulting probability of .2 is not significant, but when, as shown, the 60-100 group is further divided at the 80th percentile, some support may be found for the hypothesis that the sheep-goat classification is most effective for subjects who have a strong interest in theoretical problems.[2] A further testing of this idea is a project for the future.

Conclusions

What conclusions can be drawn, then, after nine years of asking more than thirteen hundred ESP subjects, with varied phrasings, whether they accept the possibility of paranormal success under the conditions of the experiment? First, the data point to the fact that, under the conditions of these experiments, attitude toward the experiment has a relationship to ESP scores. Those subjects who had a favorable attitude tended, on the average, to score above the level of mean chance expectation. Those with an unfavorable attitude tended, on the average, to score slightly below mean chance expectation. One may suppose that among the latter group many of those who recognized the statistical problems involved in the research tried (perhaps unconsciously) to obtain "chance" scores; but that many of those who were naive with regard to the statistical problems aimed (unconsciously) at avoiding the assigned target; and thus the group as a whole tended to obtain scores lower than mean chance expectation.

Second, from a priori argument, from the weakness of the sheep-goat effect as we found it, and from a comparison of our data with those of others, one may reasonably infer that many variables, in addition to acceptance of the possibility of paranormal success,

2. Errors in the original publication of these data [Schmeidler, 1952a] have been corrected here. The original paper claimed a significant sheep-goat effect as well as an interaction with the theory-interest classification. When the data are analyzed by the more appropriate method of Table 18, only the sheep-goat effect reaches significance. Relevant statistical criticisms [Burdock, 1954] of the original article are believed to have been met in the present treatment.

help to determine the subject's attitude toward the experiment, and that a single question, which emphasizes a single aspect of the problem, gives only a partial picture of his attitude. No single question, therefore, is likely to be a very good indicator of ESP success.

Third, a comparison of our results with both the successful and unsuccessful work of other parapsychologists suggests that the interpersonal relations between subject and experimenter, and hence both the population of subjects and the personality of the experimenter, are important to the pattern of the ESP effects that will be obtained. Conversely, although it is dangerous to generalize from one population to another, it is likely that large groups of subjects drawn from a common "cultural climate" who go through a standardized, similar procedure with one experimenter will show ESP score consistencies from one group to the next.

CHAPTER 7

The Rorschach Test and ESP Scores

BECAUSE there were so many individual exceptions to the hypothesized sheep-goat relationship, it became clear that there should be a systematic study of personality variables other than intellectual acceptance or rejection of the possibility of paranormal success in the experimental situation. We hoped that projective tests and particularly the Rorschach would differentiate successful ESP scorers from the unsuccessful. All subjects after the first three series (Table 3) were requested to take personality tests in addition to the ESP test. Much of the remainder of the book will be devoted to an account of what was discovered from these tests. It is —even more than the description of sheep-goat differences— an account of the unfinished business of our research, of methods and attempts which have not entirely failed, nor yet succeeded to the point of providing a stable foundation upon which to build.

The Rorschach test [1] was administered to more than 1000 subjects in classroom groups. In addition there were a few indi-

1. The Rorschach test, devised by Hermann Rorschach in the decade before 1921, is a clinical tool for the assessment of both normal and abnormal personality. The test consists of ten standardized cards containing meaningless ink blots, some in black and white and some in color. The person taking the test is asked to look at the cards one at a time and to say what the ink pattern seems to resemble.

Records are susceptible to formal analysis in many different aspects. What was the total number of responses to the ten cards? What percentage of responses used an ink blot in its entirety rather than a portion? Were the conceptions far-fetched or life-like, animate or inanimate, human or animal, moving or still, common or unusual? Each response can be categorized in these and other ways, and the relative or total number of responses in particular categories can be compared to statistical norms for various populations.

In a loose sense the Rorschach measures "imagination," but it obviously tells much more. The subject is given an unstructured task and asked to make of it what he will; his resulting behavior will reflect many facets of his personality.

The Rorschach is so widely used that it has acquired a jargon, which may be mystifying, attractive, or repelling, depending upon the layman's temperament. Behind the language, however, is an earnest and partially successful attempt to deal with a difficult scientific problem—the understanding of human personality.

vidually administered records, which will be described separately in the last half of this chapter.

The classroom Rorschach records were scored in three ways. Two of these depended upon Munroe's [1945] "Inspection Technique," the third upon an earlier Rorschach method.

The Munroe technique is based upon the Klopfer scoring procedures [Klopfer and Kelley, 1942]. In Munroe's method an "adjustment score" is obtained by totaling one or more checks which may be assigned in each of 27 scoring categories to indicate roughly the degree of deviation from a norm. Munroe had found at Sarah Lawrence College that student adjustment scores were related to academic success. Relatively well adjusted students were more able than the poorly adjusted to use their ability to achieve their goals.

In applying this concept to the present research, it was reasonable to assume that in general the sheep would want to succeed in their ESP guesses, but that goats, despite a superficial willingness to cooperate, would be motivated to "disprove" the ESP hypothesis. If better adjusted subjects are more able to achieve their goals, we should expect that the well adjusted sheep would make higher ESP scores than the other sheep, and that the well adjusted goats would make lower ESP scores than the other goats (if some of the goats were statistically naive and tried for scores as low as possible). Thus the sheep-goat difference would be greater for the well adjusted subjects than for the others.

This hypothesis was supported by a preliminary analysis of the Rorschach and ESP data [Schmeidler, 1947, 1949, 1950a] and, more recently, by an analysis of variance in which the subjects were classified as sheep or goats and as either well or poorly adjusted. It had been originally planned to present these data and their analyses in this book. More detailed study has revealed an unexpected discontinuity in ESP performance as a function of the Munroe adjustment score. Because of this unanticipated finding, we are reserving a full account of the data on adjustment for later publication.

The second method of scoring the Rorschach records used a list of seven empirically prechosen "signs" to select a group of subjects in which the sheep-goat effect was most pronounced. Here also an analysis of variance for the test group confirmed at a high level of significance the hypothesis developed from the preliminary group: that the sheep-goat effect was found primarily in the subjects whose records did not show the Rorschach signs. Because most of these signs appear also in the Munroe scoring categories, the full report of these data will be published with the report on adjustment.

To avoid misinterpretation of the sheep-goat data, it seems necessary to anticipate this full publication by a brief statement of GRS's conclusions from the Rorschach analyses.[2] The absence of sheep-goat differences in the predicted direction among subjects with poor adjustment, or among subjects who show certain Rorschach signs, indicates to GRS that an intellectual attitude toward ESP (which is the basis for the sheep-goat dichotomy) will be almost irrelevant as a behavioral determinant for subjects whose social adjustment is poor or whose needs and response tendencies show certain marked deviations from the average. This, of course, would be anticipated by organismic or field theories of behavior. The procedural corollary of this proposition is that there are many populations and many environmental settings in which we cannot expect the sheep-goat question to have the same bearing on ESP scores that it has in our own subjects—that is, in a group of fairly well adjusted college students, tested in an atmosphere which was conducive to good will and not antagonistic to ESP.

The third method of analyzing the group Rorschach records used a rescoring according to Rorschach's directions and is tentatively presumed free from whatever distortions there may be in the Munroe scoring. The results are of only marginal significance and the method is reported here as a guide to further research.

In his original publication, Rorschach [1942] described certain measures or ratios which offer a quantitative summary of the personality pattern. We shall present evidence suggesting a connection between ESP scores and Rorschach's most important ratio, the "experience type."

Rorschach, in his description of experience types, discusses four

2. It is RAM's judgment that no unique and wholly convincing explanation has been found for the above-mentioned data discontinuity, and hence that there is in the data no sound statistical evidence to support the adjustment and sign hypotheses here under discussion.

extreme possibilities: coartative, ambiequal, introversive, and extratensive. The first two are roughly equivalent to overrepressed and well balanced; the last two may seem self-explanatory, but in fact have somewhat different connotations from the terms "introvert" and "extrovert" that are now so commonly used. Since only the first two appear to tie in with differences in ESP scoring levels, they will be defined more carefully, and the others will be omitted in the ensuing discussion.

The operational definition of these terms, as they are used here, is that the coartative subject is one whose protocol [3] has no more than one M (human movement response) and one C (moderately strong color response). (This follows Rorschach's usage.) The dilated ambiequal subject is one whose protocol (a) has at least five M and five C, but (b) does not have twice as many C as M, and (c) does not have twice as many M as C. (This departs from Rorschach's usage, since we are reserving the term "dilated" for those ambiequal protocols where there are five M and five C, or more.)

What do these categories connote? Rorschach characterizes the coartative normal individual as one who "demonstrates his ever-present mastery of his conscious functions over all his living, whether it be subjective life, or in the world outside himself"; and he characterizes the contrasting group, the normal dilated ambiequal individuals, as those "in whom are combined marked introversive features including creativeness, subjectivity, and intensive rapport, with marked extratensivity, as shown by extensive rapport, ability to make sympathetic reproductions, excellent emotional approach, and motor adroitness." We may take this to mean that the coartative subjects are expected to be highly controlled and somewhat withdrawn, and that the dilated ambiequal subjects are expected to be both interested in, and responsive to, the situations in which they find themselves.

ESP scores of sheep and goats who were dilated ambiequal or coartative are listed in Table 19. The dilated ambiequal subjects had mean scores slightly above chance expectation; the coartative subjects had mean scores slightly below. The difference is suggestively significant at the .05 probability level, without correc-

3. In psychology the "protocol" is the original record of experimental results, made during the progress of or immediately upon the conclusion of an experiment.

tion for neglect of the other experience types. Let us therefore propose as a hypothesis for future test that dilated ambiequal subjects will tend to make higher ESP scores than coartative subjects. It should be noted that what is predicted here is a "main effect"

TABLE 19. ESP SCORES OF DILATED-AMBIEQUAL AND COARTATIVE SUBJECTS
(An Exploratory Computation Based upon These Categories within All Subjects Rorschach-Tested by Schmeidler, 1943 to 1951)

	DILATED AMBIEQUAL		COARTATIVE	
	Sheep	*Goats*	*Sheep*	*Goats*
Subjects	23.	17.	35.	28.
Runs (of 25 guesses)	213.	152.	302.	247.
Mean run score †	5.23	5.17	5.07	4.77

	VARIANCE ‡	d.f.	*t*	P
Pooled variance among all subjects	3.956	99	—	—
Sheep vs. goats, main effect §	10.2	1	—	—
Dil. ambi. vs. coartative, main effect §	16.1	1	2.02	0.05
Interaction	3.1	1	—	—

† *Chance expected value is 5.00.*
‡ *Chance binomial variance is 4.00.*
§ *Ignoring slight disproportion of subclass numbers.*

and not an interrelationship with the sheep-goat classification. Any theoretical interpretation of this hypothesis, beyond that implied by Rorschach's description of the terms "coartative" and "dilated ambiequal," can well be left until validation has been achieved.

The chief virtue of the Rorschach as a diagnostic instrument is not that it gives a list of separate scoring categories but rather that the subject's protocol, taken as a complicated whole, suggests a picture of the balance among the subject's diverse response tendencies; of his abilities, character structure, worries and desires, and the way they interact. Unfortunately, the very subtlety of the Rorschach that makes it effective as a clinical tool also makes it unmanageable as a whole for quantitative scientific research, or at least, provides a challenge to which we have not been equal.

In the remainder of this chapter we shall describe a cooperative effort to use the Rorschach as the psychiatrist might like to use it for the determination and understanding of ESP ability. For this purpose the group Rorschachs lack sufficient precision and detail. Early in the research, however, some individual protocols had been obtained. They were submitted for comment to two Rorschach experts, each of whom analyzed some records and then consulted briefly with GRS, either in conferences or by mail. The analyses were made on different records and were independent of one another. The resulting comments, reported below, do not seem at variance with our findings, and in some instances are strikingly similar.

Early in 1945 Zygmunt Piotrowski generously agreed to donate some of his time and skill to parapsychological research. Since the time that he could volunteer was necessarily limited, we agreed on the following plan as being the most economical in hours and the most challenging for him.

From the ESP subjects who had taken individual Rorschachs, GRS was to select some who had very high ESP scores, some who had ESP scores very near the level of mean chance expectation, and some who had very low ESP scores. Their Rorschach protocols were to be typed out, shuffled, and sent to Dr. Piotrowski, without any notation concerning their ESP performance. He was then to attempt to group them on the basis of similarity of Rorschach patterns (and his own impression of the patterns that were relevant to ESP success) and to let GRS know what the grouping was. If his grouping showed only a chance resemblance to the groupings of ESP scores, the trial would be considered a failure and he would regroup the records on some other basis. If, however, his groupings showed a close resemblance to the original ones, he would describe in detail the criteria he had used in making up his categories. In accordance with this plan, Dr. Piotrowski examined fourteen Rorschach protocols, and divided them into two groups: above chance on ESP, and at or below chance. On the third such division, ten records were correctly placed. Without a confirming repetition, these results are meaningless from a statistical point of view. But the criteria which he developed, in this last, suggestively successful grouping, deserve presentation as an encouragement to further research. In his own words:

The first attempt to formulate a hypothesis which might contribute to the understanding of an ESP-ability was based on the conventional scoring categories of the Rorschach. The basis of the hypothesis was slowly changed until it dawned on me that I might take seriously the word "perception" in the ESP symbol and that I might try to explain the difference between the above-chance and the other groups by difference in the perceptual approach to the Rorschach plates. And it was on this idea that the least unsuccessful attempt at classification of the cases was based. This was the formal hypothesis:

Traits assumed to be characteristic of the above-chance group: A greater acceptance of things (inkblots in this case) as they are, greater passivity in looking at the blots but being less challenged to observe the details and feeling no desire to "correct" them. The above-chance group produces visual images that are less determined by details and much more by the general, global, and rather vague outlines or surface values. This relative independence of details permits a greater play of the imagination. The above-chance group does not hesitate to see individual varieties of familiar objects. Its attitude is more that of an observer and/or an aesthete, permitting himself to be stimulated in order to enjoy the play of his imagination. The above-chance subjects do not approach the blots in the spirit of a practical man who wants to do something about the thing (inkblots in this case), improve it, or classify it according to the impersonal, rational, and common-sense system of practical people, whose thinking is only a preparation for action, and who are not interested in mere observation or dispassionate comprehension.

Thus, the members of the above-chance group accept the plates as they are, without protest or without any reformatory ambition. They permit the plates to exert as much influence upon them as possible, but on the other hand their response is an individual one. It is a "feeling response," the sensory data being incorporated into the subjective imaginary life of the individuals. The positive reactions of the above-chance group are much more definite and are less modified by additional associations than those of the below-chance group. The verbal form in which they are expressed may change and undergo modification, but not the visual image stimulated by the plate. Additional sensory detail perceived in the process of looking at the plates elicits new ideas rather than leads to changes in the old ones. The emphasis is on the effect created by the plates on the viewer. Thus in the above-chance group there were many "symbolical" responses and many expressions of emotional attitude, such as "peace," "serenity," "wonderment," etc. Because of this impressionability the above-chance group gives many "faces" and "eyes," responses which are most likely to [indicate] impressions, generalized needs, intuitive insights without any awareness of details. Thus there is a certain degree of emotional independence in the above-chance group, a certain degree of psychological self-sufficiency, a peculiar type of mild asociability yet without much (if any) social rejection of people. The feeling of incompleteness, the reliance on certain general and hardly defined aspects of the whole, the idea that there usually exist greater possibilities than are apparent— this might be another way of describing what I think is the above-chance-group way of perceiving and responding to the blots.

The pure-chance and/or below-chance groups are quite different. They seem very much more aware of the difference between their impressions (sensations and/or interpretations) of the plates and the objective, physical easily noticeable traits of the plates. When they give their imagination free rein, they make it clear that imagination and perception are two very different processes. They are conscious that they have interpreted the blots, that the blots are not ideal in shape, that there exist marked differences between their visual images projected in the blots and the actual shape of the blots. Frequently they point out these differences obsessively. They explain their projected images in practical terms of usefulness and reasonableness. They have an engineer's approach, not that of an aesthete.

In the chance and below-chance groups there are no (or at best incidental) references to personal *feelings* or moods but there are many references to personal but actual *experiences,* observed and reported in the fashion of unimaginative reporters. They feel an urge to justify their percepts. They are apt to say that a certain lake looks just like the blot they are looking at. Thus they describe many objective details, giving few if any descriptions of their subjective feelings. Imaginative elements are frequently retracted when a more accurate perception does not seem to justify them. The chance and below-chance groups "see," and manifest no wish to experience the feeling of hidden possibilities. There is likely to be scientific sobriety.

In a separate project, Bruno Klopfer has examined the records of some ESP subjects whose scores were unusually high. He was informed that these were the records of "good" subjects, and was asked to point out any outstanding characteristics that they showed, and any characteristics that they had in common. Although he was not able to study them sufficiently to arrive at a firm conclusion, his impression was that these records showed an unusual tendency to accept, as if they were not contradictory, different interpretations of the same area. For the two subjects whose ESP performance was most outstanding, he commented that they had the "possibility of multiple personality. At one level they showed an ordinary, banal mental approach with good adjustment; and without integration, at a different level of personality, they showed a flair for the symbolic and the abstract."

The lack of integration which Dr. Klopfer remarked is reminiscent of Dr. Piotrowski's analysis. (It will be recalled that the comments were made about different subjects.) In general, the major point of similarity between the two statements was the emphasis on the fact that the high-scoring subjects permitted themselves to be stimulated in order to enjoy the play of their imagination, and felt less challenged than do most people to try to justify discrepanies, or to "correct" the details of what they saw.

Summary

The Rorschach was used both quantitatively and qualitatively in a search for ESP-personality correlates. The quantitative search, requiring a great many records, was hampered by the insensitivity of the group method of Rorschach administration, and the qualitative approach was limited by the labor of gathering and evaluating individual protocols.

Statistically significant relationships were found between ESP and adjustment (as measured by Munroe's Inspection Technique for evaluating Rorschach protocols) and also between ESP and the absence of certain Rorschach "signs." Because the interpretation is unclear, these data have not been reported here. The conclusion drawn by GRS from this material is that the sheep-goat effect does not appear in groups with poor social adjustment or with certain pronounced behavioral tendencies.

An exploratory analysis involving Rorschach's experience types points toward the hypothesis that dilated ambiequal subjects will have ESP scores above coartative subjects. Comparisons of individual Rorschach protocols and ESP performance carried out independently by Zygmunt Piotrowski and Bruno Klopfer suggest that a readiness to accept new experiences and a lack of rigidity in perception may be associated with ESP success.

No sheep-goat interaction was found in the experience-type analysis, and none could be sought in the analysis of the several individual protocols. Although integration with the sheep-goat work of previous chapters is therefore not possible, an echo of the present findings will be heard in the following chapter on cerebral concussion.

CHAPTER 8

ESP Tests of Patients Suffering from Cerebral Concussion

IS THERE A LOCUS of ESP ability, or of the processes which inhibit it, within the nervous system? One way to answer this question might be to find subjects who have had localized brain injury, to give them ESP tests, and to determine (a) if any area of brain injury is associated with high ESP scores, or (b) if any area is associated with ESP scores that show no consistent difference from a random distribution. If such loci should be found, they would presumably be functionally related to the facilitating or inhibiting of ESP response.

The most difficult part of such research is to find subjects with clearly mapped areas of brain damage. Having tried fruitlessly for some time to find such subjects who would be available for ESP experiments, we finally decided to do exploratory research with any available subjects who were known to have any kind of brain injury. All whom it was possible to test were suffering from concussion, with no signs of focal injury. Thus the experiment which was performed was not the one we set out to do, and it can give no information about brain localization of the ESP response. It nevertheless is worth reporting, because the results are statistically suggestive at the .012 probability level and because a comparison between the ESP and Rorschach data seems to throw interesting light on the manner in which ESP functions. The present account is adapted only slightly from the report that has already been published [Schmeidler, 1952b].

The basic plan of the experiment was simple. Patients suffering from brain injury were to take ESP tests and Rorschachs; the same tests were to be given to other patients hospitalized for a similar length of time but not suffering from brain injury; and the data of the two groups were to be compared with each other and, in the case of the Rorschachs, with the norms for the non-hospitalized population. Because of practical difficulties, the total number of patients examined was only 29.

The targets differed from the usual ESP material in two repects. Each deck consisted of only ten cards, instead of the usual twenty-five; and the side of the ESP card on which the symbol was printed, was painted in one of five colors (red, green, yellow, blue, or brown). The subject's task was to guess the color as well as the symbol on the card.

The target series was prepared by assigning two of the digits 0–9 to each color, and two digits to each symbol. The experimenter read off the order of the colors from a randomized list of numbers and recorded it; did the same for the symbols; and then paired the first color with the first symbol, the second color with the second symbol, and so on. A permanent written record was made for each series of ten such pairs, the corresponding painted ESP cards were piled in order, and both cards and written records were slipped into an opaque, unmarked container. A large number of these containers was available for the experiment at all times; as a result the experimenter could not identify any of them.

It was decided before the experiment began that no distinction would be made between colors and symbols in scoring, since the chance probability for a successful response is the same for both (one-fifth). Thus the list of ten painted cards was scored as if it were a list of twenty ESP symbols.

The reason for modifying the customary procedure by this introduction of color and by shortening the deck was that normal subjects quickly become bored with a long series of guesses, and it was anticipated that, in addition to being bored, hospital patients would quickly become tired. It was hoped that responding to a colored card bearing a symbol would be psychologically equivalent to a single response (just as it is hardly more difficult to read the word CAT in tachistoscopic exposure than to read the letter A) and that the patients would be hardly more fatigued by responding to both color and symbol than by responding to the symbol alone. Thus the number of responses given by the subjects would be doubled by using painted cards with, it was hoped, minimal additional discomfort.

One uncolored sample of each symbol was retained in the experimenter's kit, as were five unmarked cards (the reverse side of children's "trading cards"), each painted in one of the five colors used for the targets.

In administering the experiment, a nurse or attendant introduced the experimenter to the patient, and whenever possible put screens around the patient's bed to reduce the distractions from the rest of the ward. The experimenter explained the procedure and arranged the ten sample cards where the patient could see them. This was comparatively easy where the patient was lying on his side or could turn his head; but in some cases, where the patient was lying supine and almost motionless, the experimenter had to hold the cards above him. The patient was asked to indicate his guess about the first card, and was permitted to do so either by stating the color and symbol, or by pointing to the appropriate samples before him. The experimenter recorded each response immediately after it was made.

The opaque container holding the target was screened from the subject throughout the experiment. After the first pair of responses was recorded, the experimenter pulled out the first card and showed it to the subject.[1] The subject then made his second pair of responses, the experimenter recorded it and showed him the second card, and so on. The subjects were strongly urged to respond to ten cards, but some patients were unable or unwilling to complete this series.

After ten pairs of responses had been made, the permanent record of the targets was withdrawn from the opaque container and the subject's name entered upon it. The Rorschach was then administered in the standard manner, except for minor changes necessitated by the cramped space or the patient's disability. In some cases, for example, the experimenter held the card, and turned it as the patient requested, instead of putting it in the patient's hand.

Eighteen patients who were diagnosed as suffering from cranio-cerebral trauma acted as subjects. Ten of them completed the Rorschach; one began but was unable to complete it. Six additional subjects were diagnosed as having had cranio-cerebral trauma, but were discharged from the hospital on the day of the

1. Because of the method of preparing the decks, knowledge of success or failure on one card did not alter the probability of success on those remaining.

test. Presumably they had recovered from noticeable effects of the concussion, and their results are listed separately. Five of these took the Rorschach; one refused to take it. Five patients were tested who had recently been hospitalized for fractures due to accidents and who did not have a head injury. The ESP scores are summarized in Table 20. The data will be discussed in terms of the questions that arose in the course of the research.

TABLE 20. ESP SCORES OF HOSPITALIZED PATIENTS SUFFERING FROM CEREBRAL CONCUSSION, OF HOSPITALIZED PATIENTS RECENTLY RECOVERED FROM CEREBRAL CONCUSSION, AND OF PATIENTS RECENTLY HOSPITALIZED FOR FRACTURES WITHOUT CEREBRAL INJURY

	NUMBER OF SUBJECTS WHOSE MEAN SCORES WERE				DEVIATION	CHANCE
SUBJECTS	*Above Chance Expectation*	*At Chance Expectation*	*Below Chance Expectation*	TOTAL NUMBER OF GUESSES	FROM CHANCE EXPECTATION	PROBABILITY OF DEVIATION
Suffering from cerebral concussion	13	3	2	341	+22.8	0.003
Recovered from concussion	1	1	4	120	− 3.0	—
With fractures but without head injury	1	1	3	82	− 1.4	—
Total not suffering from concussion	2	2	7	202	− 4.4	—

Question I. Was the combined ESP score of all patients suffering from concussion significantly different from chance? Eighteen patients suffering from concussion were given a total of 341 trials and obtained a deviation of +22.8. The chance binomial probability (.003) of this deviation is significant and warrants the supposition that ESP did occur.[2]

2. A subsidiary question from the point of view of the chapter, but nevertheless one of general interest, is this: Was the ESP score of all these subjects combined,

Question II. Were the comparatively high ESP scores representative of the concussion group as a whole, or were they due to the extremely high scores of only a few subjects? Of the 18 patients, 13 had scores above chance and two had scores below. If one ignores the three scores at chance expectation, the probability of so deviant a distribution upon the 50 per cent binomial hypothesis is less than .01. It is a reasonable inference that the nonchance behavior was widely distributed among the group.

Question III. Should the high ESP scores of the concussion patients be attributed to the effects of concussion, or to other factors that characterized the group, such as having recently had a serious accident, or being hospitalized?

Unfortunately it was impossible to collect a large number of control cases from patients who had recently been hospitalized because of an accident which did not involve head injury. The second and third groups of Table 20, however, can be used to give a partial answer to our question. These patients, five of whom had recently been hospitalized for fractures and six of whom were still in bed but were discharged on the day of the ESP test, had ESP scores that were slightly, but not significantly, below the level of mean chance expectation. If we compare the 11 patients in the control groups with the 18 patients suffering from cerebral concussion, the ratio of patients above and below the expected chance average may be evaluated in a two-by-two table. By the "exact" method [Kendall, 1951, *I*, 303], and allocating the chance-level subjects equally to the above and below categories [3] while making no a priori assumption as to the direction of the effect, the chance probability of so great an interaction is .012. The control data therefore suggest that neither hospitalization nor the shock of a recent severe accident caused patients to give high ESP scores under the conditions of the experiment. We can conclude, tentatively, that the high ESP scores of the concussion patients should be attributed to the effects of the concussion.

---

significantly different from chance expectation? A total of 543 trials were administered to 29 patients, some with and some without concussion. The deviation from expectation was +18.4, for which the chance probability under the binomial null hypothesis is .05.

3. Because this computation summarizes the chapter findings, we have followed the conservative procedure of retaining the chance-level subjects. When these informationless data are omitted, the chance probability is less than .01.

Question IV. What other changes were characteristic of the concussion patients?

Two types of material are available here: observations of the behavior and comments of the patients, and analysis of their Rorschach records. Because only ten of the group completed their Rorschachs, the former is probably the more revealing.

The most noticeable characteristic of the concussion patients was their inertia and their vagueness. They typically lay quiet in bed, not reading, talking, or moving. It was often hard for GRS to judge whether they were asleep or awake, even though the nurses would state confidently that they were awake, would then speak to them, and would elicit an unstartled, quiet, mildly cooperative response. They were relaxed or inert rather than tense, even when they complained of pain; movements and speech were slow; they were passively cooperative or merely passive and silent. Typically, their facial expressions were relaxed, as in sleep; sometimes they smiled, sometimes tears came to their eyes, but they very seldom laughed or grimaced. As compared to patients suffering from fractures, they exerted themselves very little to help the experimenter arrange the materials, even when they were most cooperative.

All this is, of course, an impressionistic account, unquantitative, uncontrolled, and summarized in spite of exceptions. It is, however, consistent with descriptions given to the experimenter by the nurses, and with some of the comments in other published material [Brend, 1941; Denny-Brown, 1945].

The sparse Rorschach material does not deserve detailed quantitative analysis, because no large group of records drawn from individuals of similar age, national backgrounds, education, and socio-economic level was available for comparison. Three outstanding characteristics of the records should, however, be mentioned:

1. They were extraordinarily short. The range was from four to eighteen responses, with a median of nine. Records with nine responses are in the fifth percentile of the normal population [Cass and McReynolds, 1951].

2. The form level was unusually poor. Only 58 per cent of the responses had good form, while the lowest figure quoted for the

normal population is 70 per cent good form responses, at the fifth percentile [ibid.].

3. Although seven of the ten subjects gave some color response in the test proper, the color was integrated with an adequate form response (FC) by only two of the subjects, while six of the subjects gave responses where color was dominant over form (CF or C). The customary ratio, in the normal adult, is either more FC than CF plus C responses or else perhaps approximately equal numbers [ibid.; Klopfer et al., 1954].

The implications of these three items are consistent with the behavioral picture described above. The small number of responses and the poor form level indicate that the patients made little effort to respond and were inaccurate and uncritical in their responses to reality. The preponderance of color over form in the color responses indicates further, according to Rorschach theory, that the patients tended to respond freely and impulsively to impressions from the outer world. If this latter characteristic had been combined with a larger number of responses, and certain other factors, it might have been taken to represent the forceful, egocentric, overimpulsive behavior pattern that is likely to lead to selfish or even criminal behavior. In these patients, however, with their short protocols and poor form perception, it would seem to indicate a feeble readiness to accept and to respond spontaneously to whatever stimuli came from the outer world, no matter how illogical these stimuli appear to be. This is an interesting point to note in connection with the marked ESP success of this group of subjects. It raises the question, so forcibly presented by Ehrenwald [1948], of whether we have learned to inhibit our ESP responses because ESP is not clearly localized in time and space, and is therefore useless to us for most practical purposes; and of whether this learned inhibition has been lessened in the relaxed patients still suffering the effects of concussion.

Question V. Did individual differences among the subjects confirm, contradict, or supplement the general trend of the data?

It is of interest to examine the records of the subjects whose ESP scores were at or below the level of mean expectation, in order to check on whether personality patterns, as well as ESP scores, were different from the rest of the concussion cases. Since there were only five such subjects in this experiment, we shall describe each of them.

Mr. D, age 65, was diagnosed by the attending physician as a conversion hysteric. (Three subjects in Chapter 3 were called A, B, and C. These five will be referred to as D–H.) The physician stated that although the patient had actually suffered a concussion, he was exaggerating his disability, probably for the sake of additional benefits from insurance. This crafty game that he was playing with the hospital staff was obviously unlike the passive cooperation of the typical concussion patient.

Mrs. E was a 76-year-old woman, tested during the first month of the experiment. Later, both doctors and nurses warned the experimenter against testing any of the older patients, because in their experience at this hospital, the older patients were so withdrawn as to be uncooperative. The record of Mrs. E supports their contention, since, for example, one of her first comments was, "When you're old, there's nothing left for you." This was an unsolicited remark, not to be expected as a response to anything that the experimenter had said, and was almost her only spontaneous statement.

Mr. F, age about 60, had been injured five days before the ESP session. He gave the impression that he was impatient with the ESP procedure; tried to change one of his guesses after he had seen the card; and was very quick in his responses. This behavior, and the five-day period since his injury, suggests that the effects of the concussion had dissipated at the time of the ESP test.

Mr. G, 62 years old, was hit by a taxi. His arm and leg were broken; he had bruises and stitches on his head, and bruises on his side. The ESP test was taken twelve days after his injury. He was eager, cheerful, and cooperative throughout the test, and thanked the experimenter at the end of it. Here, also, the patient may have recovered from the effect of the concussion, although he was still suffering from his other injuries.

Mr. H, 65 years old, moaned often and complained repeatedly of his pain. When the experimenter first came to his bed, he spoke about insurance, and said, "I have no money with me." The experimenter explained that she had no connection with insurance; nevertheless, a little later he spoke about insurance again.

Still later, while making his seventh pair of ESP responses, he said, "I don't know what's in it for me."

Only one of his first 14 responses had been correct. After this remark, with three pairs of responses remaining, the experimenter offered him ten cents if he was correct on either the color or the symbol of a card, and twenty-five cents if he was correct on both. He was completely correct on the ninth pair of responses, thereby earning a quarter. It may be questioned here whether, in the early part of the session, the subject had not been better oriented to reality than had the experimenter.

While brief sketches like these do not, of course, offer a sound basis for conclusions, they can suggest tentative hypotheses, or possibilities which should be investigated if later research of a similar nature is to be done. What they indicate here is that none of the five patients who performed poorly at ESP was both co-operative and passive, as is the typical concussion case. If these findings are investigated in some other project, the experimenter should note, before the subject's results are evaluated, whether the subject's general behavior was or was not atypical; the data of atypical subjects should be evaluated separately.

Using both the Rorschach and this case material as a spring-board, we shall make an interpretation that—admittedly—goes beyond the rather slight evidence. It is that there are certain more or less typical effects of concussion, which influence both the way the world appears to the patient, and the pattern of his responses to it. The general behavioral picture is one of lassitude, feeble responsiveness, and passive cooperation. The corresponding perceptual picture (as inferred from the Rorschach) is that of a relaxed, receptive attitude, an uncritical readiness to accept what comes from the outer world. It is in marked contrast to the realistic, constructive attitude that our culture (like most cultures) tends to inculcate. As a result, the typical concussion patient is more willing—and hence more able than the typical normal, alert, reality-centered individual—to respond to the faint and apparently illogical perceptions which we call ESP.[4]

4. A recent exploratory study of the ESP performance of maternity patients [Gerber and Schmeidler, 1957] tends to support the idea that a relaxed, accepting attitude is favorable to ESP success. Eighteen new mothers who were judged to be both relaxed and acceptant of the experimental situation scored significantly above chance and above a remainder group.

A comment should be made on the similarity between this interpretation and that of Dr. Piotrowski in the preceding chapter. In 1945 Dr. Piotrowski wrote his analysis, and in the same year GRS lent his letter to a friend, who shortly before his unexpected death lent it to another friend. It was almost by accident that it was found and returned in 1952, after this chapter had been written up to this point. GRS's memory of the letter had naturally dimmed in the intervening years, but on rereading it, she was struck by the similarity between Dr. Piotrowski's interpretation and that of the present chapter. Both noted as typical of subjects with high ESP scores, in Dr. Piotrowski's words, "greater passivity in looking at the blots but being less challenged to observe the details and feeling no desire to 'correct' them. . . . attitude is more that of an observer . . . do not approach the blots in the spirit of a practical man who wants to do something about the thing." It may be of some interest that Dr. Piotrowski's comments were based on subtle, largely unscorable factors in the Rorschach records, while our concussion case evaluations came from gross Rorschach characteristics supplemented by interview material.

Summary

Eighteen patients suffering from cerebral concussion gave ESP scores that were significantly above mean chance expectation, at the .003 probability level. A control group of eleven recently hospitalized patients, who had had severe accidents but were without cerebral concussion symptoms, gave ESP scores that were not significantly different from mean chance expectation. An exact nonparametric test for independence of attributes suggests $(P = .012)$ that the concussion patients scored meaningfully higher at ESP than did the control group. On the basis of the patients' behavior and their Rorschach protocols, it is tentatively assumed that their high ESP scores were due to their less active orientation toward their physical environment and their willingness to accept passively the impressions (including ESP impressions) that came to them.

CHAPTER 9

Frustration in Relation to ESP

IN THESE ATTEMPTS to study ESP, we have had two goals, which sometimes seem to lie in opposite directions. One is to learn about the way ESP functions in the person who is being tested; the other is to do clear, readily scored, repeatable experiments in which the results do not depend heavily on the clinical skills of the experimenter.

Let us state, at somewhat greater length, the difficulty in reconciling these goals. Probably the best method of studying the way in which ESP functions for any one person (at the present state of our knowledge about ESP) would be to have, as a first step, a series of "depth interviews" with him, interspersed with psychological tests. We should hope that the subject's unique personality patterns would be revealed, so that we could learn, for example, in what situations he acts most freely and in what situations he is withdrawn, when he feels sufficiently challenged so that he is likely to do his best, when he is likely to become discouraged, and so on. The next step of the research would be to put the subject into a series of the situations known to be important to him, and to have him take part in ESP tests within those situations. The final step would be to determine whether the conditions of his ESP success or failure were predictable, according to the situation he was in, on the basis of the other knowledge about his personality.

Let us assume that the results were good—that is, the experimenter was able to predict ESP success for this subject who had been studied with much care. The experiment would not be repeatable, in any strict sense, with any other individual, since the second subject's personality patterns would be different from those of the first. Nor could the experiment be repeated with the original subject at a later period, since he would have changed in the meantime. Thus, to the extent that an experiment dealing with personality is to be repeatable, it must be blurry at the edges, smoothing out individual and temporary differences, and in consequence its findings must be more or less inaccurate for each subject and for each specific situation, even if there is some crude over-all accuracy of prediction.

Throughout our research we have been trying to make a compromise between studies that emphasize the unique individual and those that emphasize group norms. The compromise technique has consisted of relying on the results of projective tests, since they both provide objective scoring categories of a fair degree of reliability, and also offer the opportunity of making deeper and subtler studies of subcategories among the subjects, or even of individual cases. It is not always a successful compromise, of course, partly because even the best projective test is not completely reliable, and partly because this approach makes it necessary to interpret a group difference with so many reservations (because of the exceptional individuals) that the interpretation loses its force.

This chapter will report data obtained from another projective technique, Rosenzweig's Picture-Frustration Study [Rosenzweig, 1945; Rosenzweig et al., 1946], a test which has the advantages, among others, of being quick and easy to administer, and comparatively easy to score. Results were statistically marginal, and the obtained correlations were always low. The reader may find them provocative rather than satisfying, for they seem to shed some light on factors that influence ESP functioning but that are not, in themselves, strong enough to give clear-cut predictions.

The Picture-Frustration Study is an attempt to investigate how subjects believe they would respond if frustrated. Let us describe it briefly. The materials of the Study consist of twenty-four line drawings, each portraying a scene in which there are two or more persons, one of whom is undergoing what would generally be considered a frustrating experience. A balloon sketched above another character, as in a comic strip, contains the words that he or she is saying, and an empty balloon appears above the frustrated individual. The subject's task is to write, for each of the twenty-four cartoons, the first reply that comes to his mind.

The twenty-four responses may be analyzed according to several different categories, but only three will be described. They refer, not to frustration, but to the direction of the subject's aggression which may arise from frustration, and are defined by Rosenzweig as follows:

Extrapunitiveness: Aggression is employed overtly and directed toward the personal or impersonal environment in the form of emphasizing the extent of the frustrating situation, blaming an outside agency for the frustration, or placing some other person under obligation to solve the problem in hand.

Intropunitiveness: Aggression is employed overtly, but directed by the subject against himself in the form of a martyr-like acceptance of the frustration as beneficial, acknowledgment of guilt or shame, or an assumption of responsibility for correcting the frustrating situation.

Impunitiveness: Aggression is evaded or avoided in any overt form, and the frustrating situation is described as insignificant, as no one's fault, or as likely to be ameliorated by just waiting or conforming.

Normal subjects will show each of the three types of response listed above. Characterizing a subject as extrapunitive (for example) on the basis of this test therefore means only that he has shown a tendency to act extrapunitively to a somewhat wider range of situations than other subjects. The three categories refer to response tendencies, not to invariable behavior traits. To anticipate later discussion, we will add that without information as to which type of situation a subject will handle extrapunitively, etc. (information which the Picture-Frustration Study was not designed to supply) it is impossible to predict his handling of frustration in any one specific situation, such as an ESP test.

Eilbert administered this study to 49 ESP subjects, tested individually [Eilbert and Schmeidler, 1950]. His procedure was to have his subjects make five ESP runs, and then take the Picture-Frustration Study. The quantitative results are listed in the first three rows of Table 21 and are suggestive of relationships between ESP scores and Picture-Frustration scores. Eilbert's interpretation of the findings is that subjects who show little aggression to others (i.e. subjects with high impunitive or intropunitive scores) can be expected to score better at ESP than subjects who show strong, outwardly directed aggression (i.e. subjects with high extrapunitive scores).[1]

TABLE 21. CORRELATIONS BETWEEN ESP SCORES AND RATINGS ON THE "PICTURE-FRUSTRATION STUDY"

GROUP	NUMBER OF SUB-JECTS	MEAN OF SUB-JECTS' ESP SCORES †	MEAN PUNITIVE RATING AND CORRELATION WITH ESP SCORES					
			Extrapunitive		*Intropunitive*		*Impunitive*	
			Mean	*r*	*Mean*	*r*	*Mean*	*r*
Eilbert								
Sheep	45	5.20	11.7	−.379 **	5.9	+.295 *	6.4	+.250
Goats	4	—	—	—	—	—	—	—
Total	49	5.17	11.6	−.313 *	5.9	+.231	6.5	+.215
Schmeidler								
Sheep	462	5.10	11.5	−.083	6.4	+.014	6.1	+.106 *
Goats	250	4.90	11.6	−.094	6.3	+.079	6.1	+.052
Total	712	5.03	11.6	−.088 *	6.3	+.040	6.1	+.084 *

† *Per 25 guesses. Chance expected value is 5.00.*
* *Nominally significant for the null hypothesis at the level P = .05.*
** *Same at P = .01.*

A suggestive sidelight is thrown on Eilbert's results by the scores of two close friends who acted as subjects for him. They made many extrapunitive responses on the Picture-Frustration Study but had an average of 6.3 on their ESP runs, which is above

1. From a statistical point of view, some reserve must be shown in interpreting these results. The method of scoring is one in which the sum of the three scores for each subject must equal 24. Thus, in theory, the distribution of scores cannot be normal. However, at least with our data, the range of subject scores is small and their scedastic curve could be expected to show homogeneous normality.

A more important consideration is the lack of independence between the three categories, extrapunitive, intropunitive, and impunitive. For example, a large positive correlation in one column tends to be accompanied by negative correlations in the others. Thus, a finding of statistical significance in more than one column must not be construed as an independent validation of meaningfulness for the method as a whole.

mean chance expectation. Eilbert notes that they were busy at the time he persuaded them to act as subjects, that they did not want

TABLE 22. CORRELATIONS BETWEEN ESP SCORES AND RATINGS ON THE "PICTURE-FRUSTRATION STUDY" FOR STUDENTS WHO WERE MODERATELY ANNOYED BY THE ESP TEST AND FOR ALL OTHER STUDENTS
(Schmeidler's Data in the Period September 1949 to May 1951)

GROUP	NUMBER OF SUB-JECTS	MEAN OF SUB-JECTS' ESP SCORES †	MEAN PUNITIVE RATING AND CORRELATION WITH ESP SCORES					
			Extrapunitive		*Intropunitive*		*Impunitive*	
			Mean	*r*	*Mean*	*r*	*Mean*	*r*
Moderately annoyed								
Sheep	74	5.27	11.0	−.246 *	6.7	+.045	6.3	+.268 *
Goats	44	5.08	10.8	−.229	6.6	+.273	6.6	+.123
Total	118	5.20	10.9	−.229 *	6.7	+.135	6.4	+.195 *
Remainder								
Sheep	88	5.07	10.9	+.087	6.7	−.039	6.4	−.095
Goats	60	4.84	11.1	+.029	6.4	−.014	6.5	−.041
Total	148	4.98	11.0	+.059	6.6	−.019	6.4	−.077

† *Per 25 guesses. Chance expected value is 5.00.*
* *Nominally significant for the null hypothesis at the level of P = .05.*

to go through the procedure at that time, and that they were extremely extrapunitive *to him,* before, during, and after their sessions, presumably exaggerating whatever aggressive tendencies they felt. He speculates that this emotional release cheered them up, and that it accounts for their above-average ESP scores. Perhaps the opportunities for freedom of expression which an experiment affords should be taken into account, as well as punitive tendencies of the subject, so as to find if the extrapunitive subject who feels he must be polite to the *experimenter* may be so much the more aggressive to the *experiment.*

Eilbert's findings prompted GRS to re-examine the scores of all her own ESP subjects who had previously taken the Picture-

Frustration Study, and to give this test to all later ESP subjects, to see if their data were consistent with his. Slight modifications of the recommended method of administration were necessary for the classroom tests [Schmeidler, 1950b].

The lower half of Table 21 shows the product-moment correlations between ESP scores and extrapunitive, intropunitive, and impunitive ratings for GRS's 712 subjects who took the Picture-Frustration Study. The trend follows that established by Eilbert, but the coefficients are much smaller. There are a negative correlation between ESP scores and extrapunitiveness and positive correlations with the other two categories. None of GRS's figures reaches unequivocal significance, and it would be discreet not to base any conclusions upon them. Nevertheless, in the duplication of Eilbert's patterns at a suggestive level of chance probability there is enough encouragement to warrant further study of the problem.

If these effects are real, their most reasonable explanation is that the more extrapunitive subjects can be expected to respond to any minor annoyances connected with the experiment by feeling hostility, so that (like the goats) they express negativism by avoiding the target. The more impunitive subjects can be expected to be more friendly and tolerant, to try to fit in with what the experimenter wants, and (like the sheep) to try to score well.

But if this explanation is valid, why are these effects so small? Probably because ESP is operating weakly in these data and the scatter of scores represents almost entirely chance causation. In part, however, the paucity of observed effects may be the result of the limitations of the Rosenzweig technique. No normal person is consistently extrapunitive or intropunitive or impunitive; he will vary his response according to the situation. The Picture-Frustration Study may delineate a general response tendency; to know what response pattern will appear in a given experiment, we must know how each subject regards the experiment.

Two examples may serve to illustrate this point: "I" was a forthright young man who was highly extrapunitive. On our general hypothesis, we would expect him to show hostility to the experiment and to have a low ESP score—except that he thought the experiment was fun. He had great vitality and zest; making these guesses was a game for him, and he liked games. When frustrated he was usually extrapunitive; but apparently he was not frustrated at all in taking the ESP test, and his ESP score was high.

J, a girl with a high extrapunitive score, was in perpetual revolt against authorities, conventions, or restrictions. (On the first card of the Rorschach she saw a man saying "Open Sesame!" while a mountain wall opened before him.) ESP represented to her, according to her comments, a defiance of intellectual restraint; and it aroused her enthusiastic interest. Her ESP score also was unusually high.

Thus these subjects, both highly extrapunitive, whose ESP scores seemed at variance with the others, were basically consistent with the rest. They were friendly to the ESP task; they did not find it frustrating; and their ESP scores were above mean chance expectation.

It would therefore be desirable that, where the Picture-Frustration Study was used to predict behavior in a specific situation (as in this experiment), it should be used concurrently with some other test which would show to what extent the situation was frustrating. Subjects who seem not to have been frustrated should be omitted, since in this situation the Study would not apply to them.

One further reservation must be made. All normal subjects will give some extrapunitive responses on the Picture-Frustration Study. Translating this into behavioral terms, we can say that under severe enough frustration, even the most long-suffering normal subject will show overt hostility. To the extent that an experiment is so frustrating that it necessarily antagonizes the subjects who take part in it, Picture-Frustration ratings (of punitive tendencies) will again fail to discriminate among them. Extremely frustrated subjects should therefore be omitted, also.

Having gone through this reasoning about the limitations of the Picture-Frustration Study in the early summer of 1949, we modified the procedure of four subsequent semesters of experimentation in an attempt to take it into account [Schmeidler, 1954]. During the standard ESP session a new group of tests was introduced. Their purpose was to provide annoyance ratings: to measure the degree of the subjects' frustration during the experimental hour. The new hypothesis was that data from the Picture-Frustration Study had little or no prognostic value for (a) subjects who were intensely frustrated or for (b) subjects who were not frustrated at all. Therefore it was the subjects who were rated as moderately annoyed during the session when they took the ESP test who were expected to show a positive relationship between ESP scores and impunitive scores, in the Picture-Frustration Study; and this same group of subjects was expected to show an inverse relationship between ESP scores and extrapunitive scores. The argument was developed and written for publication before the new series was begun.

Three methods were used to determine the subjects' frustration, or their "annoyance ratings." The first was a simple questionnaire. After each unit of fifty guesses, the subjects were asked to write at the bottom of their lists whether they felt relaxed, stimulated, or annoyed while making their responses, or whether they reacted in some other way.[2]

The second technique, on which we depended most heavily, was a variant of the incomplete sentence list described by Rotter, Rafferty, and Schachtitz [1949]. It was changed and supplemented so that the incomplete sentences would have more relevance to the ESP situation. The third indication of annoyance came from the subjects' answers to the question of whether they were sheep or goats. The alternatives had been put to them at some length. They were encouraged to make a clear-cut choice, and then to write an explanatory paragraph describing their reason. The length of the paragraphs and the vehemence with which ideas were expressed showed considerable variability.

In Table 22 are listed the correlations between ESP scores and three punitive ratings from the 266 subjects who took the Picture-Frustration test between September 1949 and May 1951. For the subjects who were rated as moderately annoyed by the ESP experiment, the correlations are in the direction predicted before the subjects were tested. Although absolutely small, the correlations are relatively large compared to those obtained with the Picture-Frustration Study alone (Table 21). However, because

2. During the three semesters beginning February 1950 and ending May 1951, GRS gave this questionnaire to 216 students. As a separate method of investigating ESP performance the questionnaire was not significantly successful. There was a negligible interaction with the sheep-goat effect, and the variance among the four categories of mood failed to reach the .05 probability level when tested against the variance among subjects.

the number of subjects is smaller, the correlations are still only marginally significant.

The analysis presented in Table 22 was arranged for the hypothesis under test. Exploratory examination shows that, after correction for sheep-goat disproportion, the moderately annoyed subjects scored higher at ESP than the remainder, with a difference probability of less than .02. This unanticipated finding presents a problem which might repay further investigation.

Summary

The research results reported in this chapter are of marginal statistical significance, but the patterns are consistent between two experimenters and are strengthened by supplementary measurement suggested by psychological reasoning. Hence, we may place a fair degree of confidence in the meaningfulness of the following findings.

When subjects were classified by Rosenzweig's Picture-Frustration Study, their ESP scores correlated positively with impunitive and intropunitive ratings and negatively with extrapunitive ratings. The observed correlations were stronger among those subjects who, by independent measurement, were rated as moderately annoyed by the ESP experiment. The simplest inference to be drawn from these findings is that, on the average, subjects who have friendlier attitudes to the ESP task are likely to have higher ESP scores than those who are more aggressive and are hostile to it.

CHAPTER 10

How Common Is ESP?

WE SHALL deal, in an exploratory fashion, with some problems relating to the experimental emergence of ESP. The title of this chapter is a popular question to which a wholly satisfactory answer cannot be given. By repeated experiment under specified conditions we can sometimes say that a particular person "has" ESP ability. But since subtle changes in procedure can inhibit ESP, how shall we decide that a person who does not show ESP was tested under the conditions that were right for him?

To understand the nature of the difficulty, we must examine the methods that have been used for detecting ESP. These tend to fall into two categories. One is the "long shot" approach, where the target is so distinctive as to be clearly identifiable: an individual's life experiences, in mediumistic material; or a picture, or word from the dictionary, in laboratory work. Here, in order to conform to the usual standards of evidence, criteria for a "hit" must be rigid. If the target is listed as an "elm tree," only an elm can be counted correct. Otherwise, if the experimenter were to give credit for an oak or mulberry, he might be tempted to call a lilac bush successful also, or perhaps anything in the vegetable kingdom, or perhaps anything elongated, or anything that was brown and green. To avoid falling into such absurdities, it is conventional to give credit only for a clear hit—if the target is a candle, to consider the response of a candle as correct, but the response of a lantern or torch as wrong [Carington, 1944].

This precaution, so necessary for the experimenter's confidence in his findings, does not do justice to the nature of ESP as it appears in Soal's work and in other studies. To the extent that ESP is an integrative process, so that the response to a single item depends in part on both later and earlier ones, we can expect it to exhibit the same sort of meaningful pattern of errors that is found in perception and memory. There, transfer or figure-ground ef-

94

fects, or other similar relationships, result in predictable inaccuracies of the subject's responses. If then, we are using a method of studying ESP where success can be scored only when there is unequivocal exactitude in hitting the target, we are probably setting up conditions under which we will not observe weak ESP ability. Experience shows that this method, if used alone, is likely to lead to the conclusion that some few indivduals have strong ESP ability and most individuals have none. It is a sieve with very large holes.

The other approach which is commonly used, is the one associated with Rhine's researches, and is the method of almost all of our own ESP experiments. It depends on the accumulation of a large number of responses, which can be summed and compared with the average chance expected score worked out on the basis of probability theory. If experimenter and subjects are patient enough, and a very large number of responses are made, even ESP ability that is extremely faint can presumably be demonstrated. This should be the method of choice to answer the question of how widely ESP ability is distributed in any population.

Unfortunately it has its own difficulties, which arise from the variable quality of ESP. One test subject, for example, in trying to guess the target correctly, may misplace his guesses, responding to the target that is to follow the one which the experimenter has designated. And with a slight, controllable change in the objective conditions, but no change, so far as either he or the experimenter can judge, in his attitude to the task, he may begin responding systematically to the second target after the designated one. (See subject BS in Chapter 2.) Another subject may give above-chance response to the target only when there are sequential repetitions in the stimulus order; another may make above-chance *incorrect* calls to a certain target, but not to other targets; another may show striking changes in scoring rate according to variations in his own mood; and so on. When we consider that there may be as many idiosyncracies possible in scoring pattern as there are individuals taking the test, it is clear that we would require a flexible and wide-ranging analysis of each subject's preliminary series of responses before we could hope to know what hypothesis to test in that subject.

Moreover, keeping the subject's attitude and motivation sufficiently constant over a long series of runs would not be an easy task. Certain changes in attitude, if undetected, could invalidate the entire series. For example, if during the beginning of a project the subject were scoring higher on the first part of a run than on the later parts, and if he happened to read some of the published material [Rhine, 1952] on "scoring declines" half way through the series, and if he reacted to this information by thinking that he ought to guard against the trap of lower scores by putting extra effort into his middle or final guesses, then the trend of his first runs might vanish, and the experiment would not demonstrate the ability which the subject possessed. This is obviously only one of many possible changes that could occur during a protracted series, and it would require a high level of clinical sensitivity on the part of the experimenter to keep such changes from invalidating the research.

Another closely related difficulty lies in the fact which has been so often reported, that ESP ability seems to vary in the same individual from one period to another. Riess' subject, whose scores were listed in Table 2, offers a striking example of this. If such variations are caused primarily by physiological changes in the subject, we may be powerless to deal with them, although careful observation might permit us to diagnose and record them. If they are due to changes in the world outside the subject, connected with unknown factors in the transmission of ESP, we will probably find ourselves—in the present state of our knowledge— unable even to speculate about them. If they relate to the subject's motivation and to his response to the experimenter and the experimental situation, a preliminary psychological study of each subject may permit at least partial analysis and control.

From this discussion it must be apparent that a categorical answer to the question "How common is ESP?" is not to be expected. Nevertheless, we are not without some information regarding the incidence of this phenomenon, or without hope that more can be obtained. The statistical data of this book tell us something of the range of occurrence of ESP in our experience. And they seem to be typical of other parapsychological data gathered from unselected subjects. There is little inhomogeneity within or among our subjects—none at all of a sort that would lead one to suppose that we were dealing with two kinds of subjects, those who "had" ESP and those who did not. Moreover, in the light of the sheep-goat effect, we must be cautious in concluding that data which conform to a chance model by any single test are necessarily free of ESP. The evidence, from this research and from other sources, is inconclusive, but it is consistent with the hypothesis that psi ability is widespread in the populations that have been tested.

An analogy between ESP ability and color vision may serve to clarify this idea. Just as it was usual in the past to say that a person either had color vision or was color blind, so the early research workers in ESP felt it was necessary to work with "good" subjects and to assume that others did not have ESP ability. By now it is more usual to say that there are many individuals who do not have full color vision, but who should be called "color deficient" rather than "color blind." At high intensities of light, with a well saturated stimulus, they can respond to color differences, though they are incapable of such color responses at lower intensities or with poorer saturation. Intense emotional need may be comparable, in the case of ESP, to intense illumination in the case of seeing colors; and the ability to respond differentially to certain light wave-lengths but not to others may be analogous to the varied types of ESP ability. (It is noteworthy that BS, Soal's gifted subject, made extra-chance scores only in telepathic-type tests, when an agent looked at the cards. In clairvoyant-type tests, when the cards were concealed from the agent, BS's scores dropped to the chance level, even though he thought that the tests were of the telepathic type [Soal and Goldney, 1943]. Other experimenters have worked successfully with both telepathic and clairvoyant card arrangements.)

It is now believed that there are very few otherwise normal individuals who are incapable of seeing any chromatic distinction even under the most favorable conditions. If the situation is indeed similar in the case of extrasensory perception, the question for our attention would seem to be not "Who has ESP?" but "How is ESP manifested?"

In searching about for ways to uncover concealed ESP, we have spent some hours in a preliminary experiment. The subjects were volunteers, each of whom previously had had a group ESP test and had taken the Rorschach and the Picture-Frustration Study.

Each subject was now given one experimental session in which he made 10 ESP runs (of 25 guesses each), and also was asked to state, just before each run, what score he expected to attain.

Our purpose in holding these sessions was to explore the possibility that analysis of the Rorschach and Picture-Frustration protocols of a subject would allow prediction of the conditions under which that subject would make high or low ESP scores. The experimenter made her clinical prediction before the subject came into the office, and then tried to set up appropriate moods or attitudes to test it. Thus the psychological part of the procedure was loose, as befits an exploratory experiment. The ESP target lists were prepared in the usual way and were concealed until the subject had completed his responses. The experimenter's impression is that five of seven subjects gave responses similar to those that were expected. Let us give two examples to show the possibilities of this approach.

One of the volunteers, who will be called Lorna Luf, had had ESP scores very close to chance expectation in the group test; she was a goat and had had a deviation of $+2$ for six runs. Her Rorschach indicated that she would make better scores in a friendly, social atmosphere than in an impersonal one, and further (with the Picture-Frustration Study record) that she would probably be frightened by success and discouraged by failure. The experimenter therefore tried to set up a challenging mood of "Let's see if you can do it," in an atmosphere of social give and take, de-emphasizing the ESP scores while at the same time directing attention to them, saying only, "It would be nice if you could do it again," after a good score, and showing polite interest in a poor one. The experimenter spoke to the subject in a more personal way than usual, telling her that her first name was a pretty one, and, when she deprecated her family name, that she probably would not keep it for long.

The desired friendly mood seemed to be established. Although during class periods Lorna very seldom smiled, she smiled often and pleasantly during the experimental session. She spoke at length about her boy friend, and her work in the community house where she met him, and said twice that she would like to have GRS come there to get acquainted with him. She disregarded the bell which rings at ten minutes before each hour, and at the second bell (which rings at the hour, and which signaled the end of the session) said that she thought it was the first one. When she left, she forgot her handbag. And her ESP scores, in contrast to those she made in the impersonal group situation, were unusually high. The 10 scores were 6, 2, 9, 8, 7, 4, 6, 6, 10, and 7, where the chance expected value is 5. The total deviation was +15 for 10 runs, a figure which might be expected to occur by chance in about one case out of 45.

For subject M the prediction was made that ESP scores would be initially high, that they would continue high if he were successful, that they would drop if he thought he had failed, but that surface cooperation (as measured by his predictions of the scores he would obtain) would continue high even after failure. With M, the experimenter adopted for the first time the expedient of lying about a subject's ESP scores, having decided before the session that he would be told that his first four scores were high, and that his next five scores were low. Thus the prediction for M was that the average of the first five ESP runs would be above 5, that the average of the last five ESP runs would be below 5, and that M's predictions as to his scores would average above 5 for both halves of the session. His obtained ESP scores were 9, 7, 3, 9, 8, 5, 3, 4, 7, 6, giving an average of 7.2 for the first five runs and an average of 5.0 for the latter five. As expected, M's aspiration levels for the ten runs were high: 6 or 7, 6 or 7, 6, 7, 7, 7, 7, 7, 7, 7; but the experimenter's ESP prediction was only partly right.

Scanty data of this sort can lead to one of two conclusions: that the results are sufficiently in line with the predictions to justify continued and more careful research, or that they are not. At best they are preliminary work, which needs to be followed by extensive further series.

This general method of clinically feeling out a technique before attempting a statistical exploration is painfully slow, and is probably foreign to most experimenters of quantitative persuasion. That it is not an entirely unsuccessful method is shown by the results reported in this book. But as an approach to the problem of how psi appears in a population, it has limitations. Among these is the absence of criteria for selecting outstanding subjects.

The reports of other experimenters show that selected subjects have maintained, for many runs, average ESP deviations ranging from 40 to 270 per cent above mean chance expectation. Thus the scores which have been found with gifted subjects are of a different order of magnitude from the average scores obtained in our research. It has often seemed that our plodding experiments, where relatively small and relatively consistent differences are studied so long that their cumulative effect finally becomes significant, are like studies of growth which examine only the relation between nutrition and height. Such studies could be pursued at great length and with great variety, one long-term research being concerned with the effect of calcium, others with each of the vitamins, and so on. And an investigator might, after many years, have a smug satisfaction because he thinks he is rounding out a complete picture of the factors involved in growth—until he runs into a pituitary giant.

Even though some degree of ESP ability may eventually be demonstrated in all, or nearly all subjects, there is evidently a higher level of such ability possessed by only a few (and probably by those few for only a part of their lives)—a level which is so much higher than the usual one that (like the eidetic image compared to the primary memory image) it is convenient to think of it as a different function. If this type of ability exists—and we believe it does—our methods are presumably inadequate to give even a hint about its basic characteristics.

CHAPTER 11

Tentative Conclusions,
and Further Problems

IF OUR ESP FINDINGS were to be summarized in a single sentence, it would state that differences in ESP scoring level were found in relation to certain independently measured psychological variables, and that in one case these ESP differences attained a high degree of statistical significance.

Though literally true, such a statement might create the false impression that the variables associated with high or low ESP scores in this research should be universally so associated. Any conclusion stated so broadly omits a crucial factor: the social atmosphere set up by subject-experimenter interaction, which we believe to be an important determinant of the way in which the personality patterns will influence the subjects' responses.

As a consequence, it is both difficult and time-consuming to conduct adequate ESP experiments. The investigator who wishes to repeat our work must be willing to take a large enough number of cases so that he can go through both a preliminary and test procedure. He should not necessarily expect to find that all of the personality traits which were associated with poor scores in our research will also be associated with poor scores in his own. He should, instead, examine his subjects' records to find the pattern that seems to differentiate good scorers from poor ones; and then repeat the experiments under as uniform conditions as possible (that is, trying to build up the same kind of rapport that he had previously) to see if the same personality syndrome will again differentiate good scorers from poor. We should expect him to find that this syndrome was different from the one which we found, if his subjects were more intensely interested or more enthusiastic than ours had been; or if they were less aware of the intellectual implications of their responses; or if he, whether deliberately or unconsciously, made most of them feel bored with the experiment, hostile to it, or extremely tense and ego-involved. The most one could hope, then, is that his own results should be consistent from one large series to another.

If such research were done, it would be desirable to go one step further. If the experimenter's personality, and the subjects' responses to it, could be studied objectively, perhaps by still another experimenter, one might find that the relation between the subjects' personality patterns (as related to success and failure in ESP) and the rapport existing between subject and experimenter was a meaningful one, and was likely to be stable from one experiment to the next. One could conclude, then, "With such-and-such type of experimenter, and with such-and-such procedure, such-and-such personality traits of the subject are positively related to high scores. With this other specified type of experimenter, under these other specified conditions, these different personality traits of the subject are positively related to high scores."

This may be a disappointingly limited conclusion, or may point to a forbiddingly difficult research program. But if it is correct, stating it will at least have the negative virtue that it will keep us from looking for uniformities where none should perhaps be expected.

The following conclusions from our data must therefore be taken, not as general truths, but as statements of personality relationships for the situations in which the experiments were performed.

> 1. Those of our subjects who accepted the possibility that ESP could occur under the conditions of the experiment (sheep) had higher average ESP scores than those subjects who rejected the possibility (goats). This effect was found among subjects tested both individually and in classroom groups, using a concealed-target (clairvoyant) technique.

The foregoing effect occurred with null-hypothesis probabilities too small to be reasonably attributed to chance. By contrast, the following findings from our research have a more tentative status, although some occurred in repeated experiments. It will be noted in this remaining work that the sheep-goat differentiation did not prove to be of importance. (For chapter references and the chronological interrelationship of the several hypotheses, the reader may refer to Appendix A, Table A-1.)

2. Among Rorschach's "experience types," the dilated-ambiequal (well balanced) subjects seemed to have ESP scores above the coartative (overly repressed) subjects.

3. And when the Rorschach protocols of several subjects were reviewed as a whole by two collaborating experts, it appeared that the best ESP scores came from subjects who were uncritically and flexibly receptive to the images seen in the Rorschach inkblots.

4. A somewhat similar finding came out of exploratory tests of hospitalized patients suffering from cerebral concussion. A passive, unreasoning acceptance of impressions from the outer world is probably conducive to superior ESP performance.

5. Several psychological classifying techniques other than the Rorschach were tried but did not prove clearly successful in differentiating ESP subjects. However, as judged by the Rosenzweig Picture-Frustration Study, overtly aggressive subjects tended to have lower ESP scores, especially if they felt somewhat annoyed by the experiment; while under the same conditions, milder, impunitive subjects tended to have higher ESP scores.

In Chapter 6, we have compared our findings as far as possible with those of other workers. How much of the literature dealing with human personality and ESP has been omitted from the book? Unfortunately a great deal; for as stated in Chapter 1, we have confined our attention to the work of others that is directly relevant to our own. There are many investigations that we have not mentioned, even though they are important for anyone who wants a well rounded picture of the status of the personality problem. A typical example is Scherer's [1948] demonstration of spontaneity as a factor in ESP; another is Anderson and White's [1957] finding of higher ESP scores in the classroom when teachers and pupils have a favorable attitude toward each other than when they have a negative one. In a series of papers B. M. Humphrey Nicol has used projective drawing techniques [1946] and personality questionnaires [Nicol and Humphrey, 1953] for separating successful and unsuccessful ESP subjects. For an adequate account of all that has been done in relating ESP to personality, the reader must refer to the journals.

Some Areas for Future Research

In the preceding chapter and in this, we have stressed the complexity of the research; for we believe that an appraisal of the difficulties ahead must temper our satisfaction with the progress made up to now. The probability must be faced that all personality attributes that are measurable simply by the subject's consciously directed motor response (words, drawings, etc.) will prove to be only distantly connected with the occurrence of psi phenomena. The kinds of relationships shown by our research are too weak and unstable to be used for the preliminary selection of exceptional subjects, and too vague and complex to give rise to a comprehensive theory. In this situation we conclude that effective understanding is a long way off and that the research attack as a whole must be much broader than it is at present.

This does not mean that we advocate abandoning research on personality attributes in ESP. In Chapter 7 we have raised a question concerning a relationship between ESP and personality adjustment as measured by the Rorschach test. Such a relationship, if real, would have profound importance for analysis of group interrelations in ESP performance (where the experimenter is considered a member of the group). The question deserves further exploration and if possible, a final answer.

In a general search for new ESP-personality relationships, other populations should be intensively examined—art students, gamblers, pre-adolescents, psychotics, people from nonliterate cultures. The classroom is a highly artificial research environment; why not try friendship groups, family groups, work groups? Stress situations, whether natural or experimentally arranged, may be productive of psi effects. The ability of the specially gifted subject requires separate study, and is likely to show relationships that could not be anticipated with our data from college students. And as previously mentioned, the personality of the experimenter is an almost unexplored variable of great probable importance.

To some extent, understanding the dynamics of ESP responses will wait for, and will improve with, better understanding of general personality dynamics. When psychologists can anticipate with accuracy the progress of therapy, or job satisfaction, or marriage success, ESP findings also are likely to be more readily anticipated. But in ESP, as in psychology generally, one does not need to wait for the millennium. We know enough, or can make enough informed guesses, to undertake some research now; and it is partly by patient, careful, and apparently minor investigations that we must prepare for other insights.

Outside of personality attributes but still within the strictly psychological domain, many questions can be asked. To what extent do stimulus patterns influence our ESP responses? Work has been done which demonstrates that the configuration of the stimulus, within which the target object is embedded, helps determine response to the target [Rhine, 1952]; but this information only points the way to further questions. How far, for example, are the perceptual laws of ESP like those of visual or tactual perception?

Still another psychological question concerns the subject's conscious intention toward the operation of psi. As a rule, a person does not know whether he has succeeded or failed at ESP until he is shown his results. And from experience, both inside the laboratory and out, one surmises that ESP works best when good results are themselves desired rather than success in the psi process leading to those results. In other words, at least the momentary interest of the subject should be in guessing the right card rather than in demonstrating ESP prowess. With ingenuity we should be able to devise a controlled experiment in a real life situation in which the subject is unaware that he is being tested and the data are gathered automatically or by a concealed investigator. If preoccupation with *self* and *process* are barriers to ESP success, such a camouflaged experiment might prove "repeatable by prescription."

It will be noticed that most of our findings concern relatively long term personality traits. Our attempts to correlate short-lived moods with ESP performance have been, at best, encouraging, even though it is our belief and the belief of other investigators that affective states are of great importance in ESP tests.

It may be that the subject-experimenter relationship, upon which we have placed such stress, is largely a matter of the kind of mood which the experimenter tends to engender in his subjects. The successful experimenter might be one whose personality (or presentation of the task) evokes relatively uniform moods, which then allow the emergence of consistent ESP-personality effects. Stated in this way rather than in terms of the experimenter's more obvious personality attributes, the problem of experimenter influence will hardly seem easier, although it may call for a somewhat different attack—possibly one aimed first at the nature of moods.

In recent years a number of drugs have come into prominent psychiatric use both as tranquilizers and for the research simulation of psychopathologic conditions. Some of these drugs may be found to affect ESP performance, but it is more likely that they could be of indirect research importance by elucidating and differentiating moods [Nowlis, 1958]. Perhaps in no other area of experimental psychology will the parapsychologist find a better appreciation of both the reality and the complexity of affective states that seem to relate to ESP performance.

Doubtless every professional psychologist can think of possible experimental connections between his specialty and psi research, but an extension beyond the psychological field is also important. The finding of physiological effects associated with psi seems especially desirable. Perhaps neurosurgical (and also genetic) aspects of ESP can be opened for investigation by the animal experiments recently undertaken at the Duke Parapsychological Laboratory.

Electroencephalography is frequently suggested as providing a neurological approach to psi functioning, but at least among human subjects its research value may prove to be indirect. W. G. Walter [1953] claims that electrical brain waves have patterns statistically associated with both transient moods and relatively permanent intellectual characteristics. He believes that the EEG can sometimes show annoyance and self-control in the presence of annoyance, that it can distinguish between abstract thinkers and those who use visual images; and that by the extent of the subject's electrical "repertoire" it gives a measure of intellectual versatility and power. If these results can be duplicated in other laboratories, EEG may provide a statistical technique for the objective specification of mental structure and affective states, and might lend itself to the classification of subjects for ESP tests.

Psi phenomena transgress the bounds of psychology and challenge the concepts of physical science. It is appropriate therefore, that physical methods be brought to bear upon these phenomena. Can the burgeoning field of information theory be of use to parapsychology? For a given average score we can compute the amount of information transmitted from a deck of cards by ESP, but is the channel-noise concept applicable? Certainly, the engineer does not seek a statistical solution when his telephone circuit is interrupted by low-frequency, nonrandom switching. On the other hand, it is "information" in the technical sense that we are dealing with in all of our ESP research, and we would be wise to follow developments in this area.

Psychokinesis, the cognate of ESP mentioned in Chapter 1, has been demonstrated upon falling objects such as dice. Most of the published papers concern wishing for a particular die face to come uppermost. More recently there have been successful attempts, notably by Forwald [1957], to displace dice laterally in their fall. It is obvious that many other matter arrangements should be tried. One thinks at once of unstable electronic circuits whose rest condition is determined randomly by thermal noise. And perhaps solid-state physicists can propose electron trigger mechanisms in crystal lattices that will yield a random macroscopic response suitable for statistical analysis.

Enough is now known from ordinary physical laboratory experience, and enough was attempted in the last-century investigations of psychic phenomena, to lead us to expect that no single, bright idea for a detector apparatus will provide the needed breakthrough in parapsychology. The obstacles to dependable performance seem to be primarily psychological and to rest in the individuals who have a psychological association with the experiment. Nevertheless, it is reasonable to hope that some matter configurations may be more easily controlled than others. As yet no systematic attempt has been made to explore these possibilities.

There is a mind-brain hypothesis of obscure origin [Eccles, 1953, pp. 261–86; Thouless and Wiesner, 1947] that lends itself to what little is known about ESP and psychokinesis. According

to this hypothesis, ESP and psychokinesis are the normal modes of interaction between a person's "mind" and the neurones of his cerebral cortex, while psychokinesis and ESP as observed in the laboratory are "leakage" effects between the mind and the outside world. Even without attempting to evaluate the merits of this hypothesis, we can use it as a source of research ideas. For example, it would be worth while to set up neurochemical models as targets for psychokinesis. Again it must be remarked that the target model would be only half the problem. The experimenter would need subjects who might reasonably be expected to exhibit psychic ability under the psychological conditions of the test. Without such subjects a negative conclusion, drawn from negative results, could have a misleading influence upon future research.

Conflicting evidence exists as to whether the paranormal response represents one general ability or whether there are different modes of operation here, just as there are different modalities for responding to sound waves and light waves. Are clairvoyance and telepathy (p. 2 n.) separate functions? Is psychokinesis as different from them as muscular response is different from perceptual response? When we can answer questions of this nature, we shall be much further along the road to an understanding of psi phenomena.

But is some practical utilization possible now? This question is often asked; we think the answer may be "yes." There are individuals exceptionally gifted in ESP. Some were described in Chapter 2, and the research literature of the field tells of many more. There is no reason to doubt that under proper conditions such persons could furnish information of a needle-in-the-haystack variety—information that is difficult to acquire by ordinary means but once found can be unequivocally validated.

Let us choose an example problem from physics. In the investigation of what is known as "nuclear quadrupole resonance," the experimenter may search the radio spectrum for days to find a weak response occurring at an unknown frequency which is characteristic of both a certain atom and the molecule to which it is attached. Once found, the frequency is published and can be easily observed by anyone with the proper equipment. Could an individual who has a consistently high rate of success at guessing

ESP cards use the same ESP ability to shorten the preliminary search of the radio spectrum?

The chemist will think of many similar problems in molecular structure which might be suitable for psychic solution. Imagining problems will be easy, and people who have had dramatic spontaneous psychic experiences can be found in any city; the real task before us is to develop clinical techniques for handling the psychic sensitive in such a way that he can produce results upon demand.

Is this a completely unrealistic proposal in the present state of our knowledge? We think not; for it is probable that at least once before, ESP has obtruded itself into the physics laboratory—albeit in an unwanted fashion.[1]

To explore all of these possibilities will require investigators with specialized knowledge in various areas. But more than that, it will require an expansion and re-orientation of the investigative effort as a whole. We should encourage an accelerated shift of emphasis in psi research away from proof-of-occurrence and toward development-of-pattern. If this allows relaxing of experimental precautions in certain directions, it also demands a raising of professional standards in others.

In parapsychology, more than in well established fields, there is need for understanding of the philosophy of science. This means, very simply, a grasp of the common core of historically successful method and a critical appreciation of the variations in method that are accepted with more or less equanimity in the several areas of science.

1. Latimer and Young [1939] published a retraction of their successful verification of magneto-optic measurements made previously by Allison. Concerning their visual observations, made at low light intensities, they said "Our initial readings appeared to set a pattern which was then reproducible. The observer had no knowledge as to the scale reading, so apparent reproducibility was due either to coincidence and would have disappeared when a sufficient number of readings were taken, or was due to some unknown mode of communication between the observer and his partner who recorded the scale readings and operated the trolley settings. In order to eliminate the possibility of inference from the tonal qualities of the voice, we used a system of buzzer signals as a means of communication. This, however, appeared to have no effect upon the reproducibility of the readings. We are inclined to question whether, under the conditions of these experiments, reproducibility has any physical significance when one member of the pair has knowledge of the previous result. Whatever interpretation one cares to make of this statement, it will at least be granted that this is a safe assumption to make in future observations of this character."

In the research itself there must be a more sophisticated use of mathematical statistics: a better knowledge of its technique, to be sure, but also a better understanding of its methodological role—for the most elegant mathematical analysis is not always the shortest route to scientific knowledge.

These are some of the problems and technical prospects of parapsychology. There are also its universal aspects, on which we as experimentalists are not qualified to write. But even experimentalists can point to the continuing need to revise our broad ideas of the nature of man and his relation to the physical world, in order to integrate our new information with what is already known. The mathematics of a universe in which ESP and psychokinesis occur, the concepts of time and causality that are consistent with precognition, the re-evaluation of our own capacities and limitations in terms of what we now call paranormal ability —these are problems which touch on many disciplines and which may stimulate our colleagues to help explore in this new field.

Plan and Chronology of Major Hypotheses

THE OVER-ALL PLAN of this research since the initial experiment (Chapter 3) was completed has been to administer both an ESP test and personality tests to the subjects, and to ascertain if relationships exist between the personality data and the ESP scores.

It does not seem likely that there is a single personality variable which stands in a one-to-one relation with ESP success. Instead there seem to be many variables, each of which may contribute some part to the complex condition in which a subject will make more hits than would be expected by chance. (This represents a problem familiar to psychologists. If we were studying cheerfulness, for example, instead of ESP success, we might find that the determining variables include the subject's digestion, his plans for the day, his reaction to the last remark that was addressed to him, and a large number of other factors.) It has therefore been GRS's practice to examine several personality variables in relation to a single set of ESP scores. Sometimes she hypothesizes that the variables interact with each other. Because of limitations both in her theorizing and in the personality tests which it is practical to administer, she does not suppose that all important variables are being studied. Nevertheless, as the years passed, the hypotheses accumulated. The later ESP tests have accordingly been related to several different personality scores. Table A-1 gives the chronology of the major hypotheses.

Throughout the book it will be noted that the number of subjects available for testing one hypothesis does not correspond to the number of subjects available for testing another. There are two reasons for this. The first is that the hypotheses were not all stated simultaneously. When, as with most hypotheses, more data per subject were needed, only subsequent subjects could be used. The second reason is that, in spite of efforts to persuade them to do so, a handful of subjects did not take all the tests. These subjects could therefore be used to help test some but not all of the theories that were currently being examined.

A critical question which is sometimes raised is whether the positive findings that have been reported can be ascribed to the

TABLE A-1. CHRONOLOGY OF MAJOR HYPOTHESES

IDENTIFICATION OF HYPOTHESIS	CHAPTERS (*Main Reference*)	KIND OF SESSION	SESSION DATES	RELATED TABLES No.	Page
Sheep and goats	3, 4	Individual	1/'43–4/'46	3– 7	33 ff.
	5	Group	2/'45–5/'51	8–11	47 ff.
Subdivision of sheep attitude	6	Group	2/'48–5/'51	16	58
"Theoretical value" (using *A Study of Values*) related to sheep and goats	6	Group	9/'50–5/'51	18	62
"Adjustment" (from the Rorschach) related to sheep and goats	7	Group	2/'45–5/'51	None	—
Seven Rorschach "signs" related to sheep and goats	7	Group	9/'45–5/'51	None	—
Rorschach "Experience Type"	7	Individual and group	9/'43–5/'51	19	69
Cerebral concussion	8	Individual	3/'50–6/'50	20	78
"Picture-Frustration Study"	9	Individual and group	8/'43–5/'51	21	88
Annoyance related to "Picture-Frustration Study" ratings	9	Group	9/'49–5/'51	22	89
Subjects' reported mood	9	Group	2/'50–5/'51	None	—

experimenter's bias in selecting cases. Let us therefore describe in detail all the instances in which data have been excluded from this presentation.

After coming to a vague decision about the general area with which a future experiment would deal, GRS often tested a few subjects informally, "playing around" with different procedures (sometimes in association with a formal experiment already under way). Data obtained informally in this way are never included in the tables and are seldom mentioned in the text. When they are mentioned, the fact that they were not a part of any formal experiment is specified.

After a formal procedure was established, all subjects who met the criteria for that procedure were included.

Where a subject did not complete an ESP run, the incomplete run has been omitted from the analysis. There were relatively few incomplete runs. All have been listed in the tabulations on file at the American Documentation Institute. Including them would have made the statistical analysis difficult, while omitting them can make no substantial difference in the findings.

Where a subject was tested as part of a formal experiment but failed to follow the instructions, his data were necessarily omitted. Some subjects, for example, after being asked to designate themselves as either sheep or goats, put themselves in one category at the beginning of the session and in the other category toward the end. Since it seemed improper to disregard either of their statements, they were left out of both sheep lists and goat lists.

If a subject took a Rorschach and stated that he was color blind, his Rorschach was omitted because it could not be scored in the usual way.

Where a subject was tested after an experiment had been formally completed, his data were omitted. This occurred inadvertently in one instance [Schmeidler, 1943b, p. 212 n.] when two subjects more than the predetermined number were tested. It occurred a few times thereafter, when a student who had been absent from class on the day of a group experiment asked to take the test, or when an acquaintance who heard of the group experiments asked to be tested. It has been GRS's practice to comply with these requests, but not to use the data.

In all, there were relatively few omissions. Decisions as to whether data should or should not be included have invariably been made without consideration of ESP scoring patterns. Where GRS knew the ESP scores before the decision was made, she described the circumstances to Gardner Murphy, who was ignorant of the scores, and asked him to make the decision.

This completes the list of ESP runs which were omitted. Several additional psychological tests were given to some subjects and several other questions were asked of the data. These showed no significant differences in relation to ESP patterns and have therefore not been included in the discussion.

Two other matters should be considered here. One relates to "optional stopping," that is, to the question of whether the experiment was terminated deliberately at a time when the results were in line with the experimenter's theory. In the initial experiment (Chapter 3) the first series was stopped when the results were suggestive (P = .03). It was then decided that additional series, each approximately the same length as the first, would be run, until the trend of the data seemed clearly to be either at chance, or extra-chance. At the close of the third series, when the cumulative sheep-goat score difference gave a probability of .005, this approach was discontinued. Thus if the research had ended with the third individual series, the criticism of optional stopping could be raised with some justification.

Obviously, however, the research did not terminate here. Instead, as more ESP data were gathered, the sheep-goat comparison was continued and other comparisons were instituted. Whenever a new kind of personality analysis seemed to give null results, it was dropped; but whenever the results seemed worth reporting, the new analysis was continued for the entire span of the experiments. Thus at the close of the project, in 1951, subjects were being formally compared with respect to their sheep-goat decision, instituted in 1943, and subdivision of sheep attitude, started in 1948; Rorschach experience type, begun in 1943; Rorschach adjustment pattern, instituted in 1945; Rorschach signs, analysis instituted in 1946; Picture-Frustration scores for extrapunitiveness, etc., first analyzed in 1948; annoyance ratings, instituted in 1949; reports on relaxation, stimulation, etc., instituted in 1950; and Allport-Vernon theoretical values scores, instituted in 1950. In short, each promising procedure was continued from the time of its inception until June 1951, when research funds from Harvard's Richard Hodgson Fellowship were no longer available for this purpose.

The data of all formal experiments of the personality series are represented in Table A-1. The final question to be answered in this context is whether there have been other formal experiments in ESP conducted by GRS during this period which were omitted because the findings were negative. Again, the answer is that there were not; but for the sake of completeness we shall describe briefly the two other experiments which she performed. In both, the targets were pictures of objects, and the subjects were instructed to respond by making drawings. One experiment was an attempt to repeat findings by Carington [1944] with this method. It gave positive results [Schmeidler and Allison, 1948] at about the same scoring level as Carington's subjects. The other, in collaboration with an Athenian investigator, seemed to him to give significant results and seemed to GRS to give suggestive results. It has never been published, since it was impossible to reach agreement on a method of evaluation. Neither experiment has any clear bearing on personality patterns in ESP scoring, and therefore neither seems appropriate for detailed analysis here.

Statistical Procedures

THE METHOD of analysis of variance has been used where possible in this book. Certain assumptions in the application of this method to our data will be discussed here. Beyond that, the reader might wish a statement concerning the statistical philosophy guiding the work, the policies adopted for exceptional data, the rules governing the presentation of results, and precautions employed against manipulational error.

Three questions may be raised concerning the application of analysis of variance to these data. The first concerns the assumptions of continuity and normality for what are presumably binomial enumeration data. The second concerns the extent to which the frequency distributions depart from the binomial (regarded as an approximation to the normal) owing to the occurrence of ESP. The third relates to the use of a common target sequence for all subjects in a single classroom, and is discussed on pages 45 and 122 and in Appendix C.

The distinction between the first two questions is important for the following reason. A logically complete answer cannot be given to the second question, but this question does not arise until one accepts the nonchance nature of the data, i.e. until one assumes that ESP or some other experimental factor is operating.[1] Hence, any reservations the mathematician may have with regard to the second question are, in their implications, not reservations

---

1. Of course it is possible to suppose that chance data do not conform to the accepted statistical models, e.g. that there is something fundamentally wrong with binomial theory even when applied to a simulated ESP experiment using digital coincidences from a random number table. This kind of speculation [Brown, 1953] is not likely to have much appeal for professional statisticians. It would destroy the statistical underpinnings of all of the biosciences—a far greater revolution than the acceptance of ESP as a new phenomenon that had somehow been overlooked in existing theories in physics and psychology. The impotence of this mathematical speculation against the experimental evidence for ESP has been discussed elsewhere by RAM [1956].

about the occurrence of ESP, but reservations as to whether (in this book) the validity of the supposed relationships between ESP and attitude (or other variable) is accurately represented by the associated probability values. Moreover, as we hope to show later in the discussion, this second question is of interest to mathematicians but not of pressing importance to the empiricist who uses statistical analysis as a tool.

The Normal and Binomial Models

Let us begin with the simpler first question, which deals with the equivalence of models. It is well known that the binomial model approximates the normal, i.e. that the distribution of the success scores obtained in a series of experiments each consisting of n Bernoullian trials with probability of success, p, approximates the normal distribution, and the approximation is better the larger n, and the nearer p to one-half. (In this book p is one-fifth under the chance hypothesis.) The analysis of variance is based on the normal model. The question of when the binomial model approximates the normal well enough to allow the analysis of variance without serious error is a mathematical question that does not depend upon the unknown nature of ESP.

For the benefit of readers without a working familiarity with the analysis of variance and the binomial distribution, several of their relevant features should be made clear. Providing p is the same, the sum of binomially distributed scores is binomially distributed. If a subject makes eight runs of 25 trials each, his data can be regarded as eight scores with an n of 25 or as one score with an n of 200. Thus, while some statisticians would question whether individual run scores are "approximately normal," most would agree that our subject-scores could be analyzed without transformation. (In the group-tested data of Chapter 5, 93 per cent of the subjects had eight or nine card runs, none had more than ten, and only one-half per cent had less than six.) Similarly, one can analyze the sheep-goat difference by lumping all the sheep scores together, and lumping all the goat scores. The total number of trials is then very large, and under the chance hypothesis the resulting total scores are normal for all practical purposes.

How do these facts fit into the analysis of variance? The run scores (whose virtual normality might be questioned) enter only into the determination of the within-subject variances (Table 4); while the variance of main interest, that between sheep and goats, involves only the clearly normal total sheep and total goat scores. The variance among subjects, which is used in the denominator of the variance ratio when testing the significance of the sheep-goat difference, depends upon the subject scores, which, as pointed out above, have a reasonably large n of about 200. Moreover, owing to the weakness of ESP effects in these data, the among-subject variance does not differ greatly, percentage-wise, from the chance binomial npq. Hence, the value of the variance ratio for the sheep-goat difference is insensitive to error (if any) in the denominator variance. The conclusion to be drawn from these several facts is that the difference between the binomial and normal models is a trivial one in its effect upon the more important findings from the analysis of variance applied to these data.

This conclusion is supported by the application of an arc-sine transformation to the data of Chapter 4. The variance values obtained from the transformed scores are within 6 per cent of those from the raw scores (Table 4). Since the raw data distribution was found to approximate the binomial rather well (Tables 6 and 7), the transformation analysis constitutes a check on the practical equivalence of the binomial to the normal distribution for analysis-of-variance purposes with these parameters and with small (ESP) variations of p from the chance value.[2]

The Data Populations

The second question raised at the beginning of this appendix is not so easily answered as the first. In the interpretation of the analysis of variance it is assumed that the data are from normally distributed populations and that variances, where pooled, have identical population values. Granted that ESP occurs, one may then ask: What are the populations being sampled, and are they homogeneously normal in the manner required?

2. It is an interesting mathematical sidelight that the theoretical run score variance from the arc-sine transformation of the binomial model is 12 per cent larger than the approximate value obtained by multiplying npq by the square of the function derivative. The latter should therefore not be used as the reference variance in a chi-square test of significance—a point that does not seem to have been made clear in the mathematical literature.

No attempt has been made to specify the populations of subjects in exact procedural terms. To do so would be to claim that these experiments are repeatable by prescription. It is hoped that others will find them so. But in the light of the history of parapsychological research, it would be unwise to claim this in advance.

With regard to most of the work, one could, of course, refer to the population of elementary psychology classes at the City College of New York, but this might prove more reassuring than meaningful. Perhaps the most important element omitted from such a specification is the experimenter who must test the students. For the population is one of data rather than of subjects, and there is much evidence to show that the experimenter is important. It would not even be definitive to refer to the senior author of this book, for she is not a fixed part of the experimental situation. In the course of a decade she has been modified by her personal history and, in particular, by her relationships to the research. One cannot say what the results might be if she were to repeat some major part of the work here presented, but one can be sure that she would no longer bring to the task her original attitudes.

The best one can attempt in the present state of our knowledge is to give as many speculative hints as possible which may help another experimenter to sample similar populations of card-guessing sessions. This has been attempted in the body of the book.

At this point the mathematician may ask, "If you are unwilling or unable to specify populations, how can you be sure that they are homogeneously normal to the extent required by the conclusions drawn?" To answer this we turn to the broader question: "How does one justify the use of the analysis of variance in any field?"

There are two sources of information available to the experimenter: past experience and present data. In some few fields, such as classical physics, the situation is so simple and our knowledge so complete that we can express our expectations in exact mathematical theories and have no need for statistical method. In other fields, such as experimental agriculture, the theory may be incomplete but our experience so extensive that we can know when to expect well behaved measurements. In still other areas, like psychology, theory may be fragmentary, repeatability difficult, and the "data source population" a highly abstract construct. In general, whenever statistical analysis is needed, our knowledge of the source population is ipso facto incomplete. Sometimes we have more information, sometimes less; but in a practical situation, rarely, perhaps never, can we say with mathematical certainty that a population is homogeneously normal.

How can we proceed if our mathematical tools have no logical finality? It is the measure of R. A. Fisher as a scientist that his method of analysis turns our attention from the hypothetical population to the observed data, and a measure of the strength of his method that it works rather well even when the data do not fulfill his mathematical assumptions. Here, then, is where we must place our confidence: what do the data show of their own statistical nature? To be sure, we must take cognizance of previous experience (regardless of whether or not it is codified in theory), and when a present sample is small, we have little else to go on but data from the past. But when, as in this book, the data are numerous, and the customary tests show them to be reasonably distributed, it is no cause for despair that, in a pioneering area, there are few prior validating measurements.[3]

Perhaps the person who rejects this point of view misconceives the function of statistical analysis as an experimental tool and has no blood for adventure. One seeks encouragement but never certainty of meaning from a small chance probability in testing a null hypothesis. Certainty comes later, from the work of others and from the growing pattern in the fabric of science. It is our hope for this book that it may contribute in a small way to the pattern of ESP, a pattern that has been slowly emerging for at least the last twenty years.[4]

3. In Chapter 10, when discussing extremely high scoring subjects, we suggested that GRS's work can be likened to studies of the effect of nutrition upon growth, and that exceptional subjects might be compared to pituitary giants. From a statistical point of view one may press this analogy a bit further. Just as the existence of pituitary giants does not destroy the reality of a finding that growth in the rest of us is affected in particular ways by nutrition, so the existence of exceptional ESP subjects, capable perhaps of producing non-normally distributed scores, does not necessarily invalidate the finding that ESP is related to "acceptance" in ordinary subjects.

4. Not all scientific authorities will agree with this. As late as 1956, P. W. Bridgman writing in *Science* [loc. cit.] has said "ESP, with its utter failure to exhibit any regularities or to perform a single repeatable experiment, is the only instance of which I am aware in which a serious claim has been made that nonchance should be capitalized [as 'ESP'] simply because it is nonchance."

Exceptional Data

The policies followed in omitting or including data are described in Appendix A. The only matter of direct statistical interest is the omission of all card runs which for one reason or another were incomplete. There were no incomplete runs in the individual series (Chapter 4) and less than three-tenths per cent incomplete in the group tests (Chapter 5). Their omission is of no consequence.

Some of the individually tested subjects (Chapter 4) attended more than one experimental session within the same series, and the data from each such subject are pooled. Three sheep appeared in each of two series. In this case the data are listed separately, and these three subjects appear in the analysis as six. The effect on the numerical results is negligible. In the ESP group tests (Chapter 5) there is no known instance where a subject was listed twice and only one instance where a subject had served also in the earlier individual series.

Presentation of Probability Values

As indicated in the Preface, we have allowed ourselves a certain looseness of expression throughout the text, as for example in referring to probability values. It will be understood, of course, that no looseness of meaning is intended. The words "probability of one in a hundred" used in describing the test of a null hypothesis are intended as equivalent to the statement that in a long series of such experiments (presumed repeatable) a score as extreme as, or more extreme than, that actually obtained would be expected to occur at an average rate of one in a hundred experiments if chance alone were operating. This statement does not assume that the ESP experiment is repeatable, but only that an equivalent, chance-controlled experiment is repeatable (equivalent as to reference variance, chance-controlled as to test variable).

In both text and tables we have used the term "variance" as a familiar landmark for the beginner even where "mean square" would be more precisely correct. We believe that the exact meaning will be evident from the context in every case.

In listing probabilities corresponding to one or two tails of a distribution, we have followed the practice of Fisher and Yates [1953]. Normal and *t*-distribution probabilities correspond to the sum of plus and minus values. Chi-square probabilities are for values equal to or larger than those observed. When comparing the variance of a superior classification with an inferior, the answer to the question "Which variable has the larger variance?" is ordinarily presumed to be theoretically known, and the area at one end of the Fisher distribution is employed. But when making a homegeneity test between coordinate classifications, the tabular probabilities have been doubled.

Because more scientists are familiar with the normal curve and the *t*-distribution than with the variance ratio, the latter has been converted to the equivalent critical ratio or *t*-value whenever possible. No confusion should arise except perhaps in the case when a variance ratio, whose degrees of freedom are both large numbers, has been expressed as a critical ratio on the normal distribution. If the test is for variance ratio known a priori to be greater than one, the single-tailed area of the normal curve is used.

The principal effect, if any, of using common targets for a classroom group (Chapter 5) is to decrease the intersubject variance. Under the hypothesis that ESP does not occur, an upper limit can be placed upon the resulting error in chance probability by testing significance against the theoretical binomial variance. If ESP is assumed to occur, the possible error cannot readily be evaluated, but from the considerations set forth in Appendix C and from the analysis of variance given in Table 9, there is good reason to believe that there would be only a negligible influence upon the associated probability figures.

Previously Published Data

In general, in reporting the published work of other experimenters, no re-analysis has been attempted and no changes made except to correct known errors. However, for the sake of uniformity all chance probability figures for sheep-goat differences of other experimenters in Chapter 6 were computed using theoretical npq and listed as approximate. Among-subject variances were not available, and experience with our own data suggests that for ordinary ESP subjects the observed variances are usually within 10 per cent of theory.

Eilbert's work, appearing in several chapters, was carried out under the direction of GRS, but has been listed separately in every case.

Where differences appear between figures in this book and in previously published papers by GRS, the present figures should be taken as correct. In part, such discrepancies arise from the omission of incomplete runs.

Procedural and Manipulational Errors

The analyses of Chapters 3, 4, and 5, of this book are based upon tabulations of data made for that purpose by GRS and now filed with the American Documentation Institute.[5] Beginning with those tabulations, the interested reader may verify the accuracy of the major tables of the book and carry out further analyses if desired.

Beginning with tabulations furnished by GRS (and filed in part, as just indicated, with the ADI) all data manipulations have been verified by repetition or otherwise. The processing of the data from tabulation to final probability values has been carried out by procedures systematically designed to minimize and detect transcription and computational errors. All operations delegated to others have been planned and closely supervised by RAM, and then independently repeated or externally verified by RAM personally.

In fulfillment of his obligation as co-author, RAM was invited to play the devil's advocate with regard to all source records of the ADI tabulations. For that purpose he spent five days in GRS's office at the City College of New York, inspecting relevant documents and reviewing experimental method. His specific objective was to find, if possible, clerical or procedural errors that might explain the extra-chance effects reported in Chapter 5. His method was twofold: to search in depth a selected portion of the data,

5. This supplementary material comes to 47 pages. Order Document No. 5456 from ADI Auxiliary Publications Project, Photoduplication Service, Library of Congress, Washington 25, D.C., remitting $6.25 for photoprints, or $2.50 for 35 mm. microfilm. Advance payment is required. Make checks or money orders payable to: Chief, Photoduplication Service, Library of Congress.

and to examine broadly the entire process leading to the final probability values.

The data selected for detailed examination are those gathered in the academic semesters beginning September 1947 and February 1951. These two semesters were chosen because they show both the highest ESP score for sheep and the greatest score difference between sheep and goats. Although they constitute only 13 per cent of the total group trials, they contribute 35 per cent of the total sheep-goat score difference.

For each subject there are two crucial items: the ESP score and the classification as sheep or goat. The documents inspected were the original record of the subjects' ESP guesses and the original statement by the subject dealing with whether he was a sheep or a goat. All of the data had previously been transcribed from these documents, via intermediate summary sheets, to the ADI tabulations. RAM's purpose was to find scoring or transcription errors.

The sheep-goat classification of these 155 subjects was checked by RAM directly from the questionnaire sheets on which the subject had described his degree of acceptance for the possibility of ESP. Cases where the subject failed to categorize himself clearly as a sheep or goat had been previously evaluated on the same sheet by GRS in accordance with the policies described in Chapter 5. RAM's task was simply that of checking between these sheets and the ADI tabulation. No errors of sheep-goat classification were found. The original sheet was missing for one subject. In this case the classification was verified by RAM by consulting the original response to a Sentence-Completion Test that had been administered between runs in the ESP test session.

The original ESP responses were checked against the original target record for all 155 subjects. In 32,650 trials there were 16 scoring errors as follows: ten cases in which a target-hit had been overlooked, resulting in a run score too small by one unit; two cases in which a target-miss had been scored as a hit; one case in which a run score total had been corrected by one unit on the response sheet, but the correction had not been carried to the intermediate summary sheet; and three cases where the subject actually made only 24 trials in the run, but his score had been treated as though he had made 25. (The failure to recognize an incomplete run gives a score bias of two-tenths, which is the expectation of score in one trial.) As a result of these errors the sheep score for these semesters, as given in Table 8 and in the ADI tabulation, is known to be too low by 7.4 (3.0 per cent) and the score difference of sheep minus goats is too small by 5.2 (1.6 per cent). These errors are negligible in their effect upon the overall result.

Detailed discussion of the actual testing procedure developed the fact that GRS was unable, after a period of four to ten years, to say whether the sheep-goat questionnaire had always been collected before the subjects were allowed to score the carbon copies of their ESP guesses. The sheep-goat questionnaire was distributed at the beginning of the class hour. The student was always asked to fill it out before the target list was revealed, and the usual rule was to collect the questionnaire with the original copy of the guesses. However, if it were not always collected, the possibility exists that an occasional subject might have delayed his sheep-goat response until after he had seen his ESP score and might have been influenced in his self-designation as a sheep or a goat by his own score, even though he was unaware of the kind of analysis which the data were to undergo.

With only this much information one might say that it is conceivable that in the case of the group-tested subjects (Chapter 5) the significance of the sheep-goat scoring difference arose from the *post hoc* classification of a few subjects. This possibility is one that might be difficult to assess in its own terms to the satisfaction of all readers. Fortunately, an answer has been found in the data of the semester of February 1951, one of the two which were rescored as reported just above.

In that semester the ESP guesses were scored by the subject on his carbon copy—not at the classroom session in which those guesses and the sheep-goat decision were made, but at the following session. The standard number of runs in that semester was eight per subject. Some subjects who were unable to complete eight runs in the first class hour and some who had been absent were given a chance to do only the last two runs at the beginning of the following class hour before the checking of the ESP scores of the class as a whole. These facts are established by the original copies of the ESP guesses and by the accompanying written description of procedure. Hence the *post hoc* classification hypothesis cannot apply to any of the first six runs of any of the subjects of this semester. These runs have been separately analyzed. Their average run score for sheep is 5.631 and for goats, 4.903. The difference in these rates is slightly greater than for all of the data of that semester. Applying an F-test to the variance of sheep vs. goats divided by the pooled variance among these sheep and goats yields a chance probability of .0010. Thus a significant sheep-goat difference has occurred under conditions where the *post hoc* classification hypothesis is known to be inapplicable.

On the Statistical Theory of Group Experiments *

Sir,—Dr. Schmeidler's interpretation of her interesting and important work reported in the November–December *Journal* seems to be marred by a statistical error. She appears to have treated group experiments, in which several percipients guess at the same target, by the same methods as she would treat individual experiments, in which every percipient has his own run of targets.

The mistake is important and it has occurred before. What Dr. Schmeidler has overlooked is that the statistics of card-guessing must be based on the question: given the guesses, how likely is it that the targets would have corresponded with them at least as closely as they do? and not, given the *targets,* how likely is it that the *guesses,* etc.? This is because we know the targets to be random, but we do not know about the randomness of the guesses. It happens that if there is only one percipient per target the statistics are the same whichever question we ask, and that is perhaps why this point has often been overlooked. But where several percipients guess at the same target it can make a great deal of difference.

A more succinct but less instructive way of putting essentially the same criticism is that we cannot evaluate the results of several subjects independently since their results are not in fact independent . . .

How can group experiments be evaluated? In theory by the use of the elaborate multiple matching methods developed by Greville and others, but in practice more simply by the almost equivalent method of getting a group opinion—e.g. a majority opinion —on each guess. Thus, if the most popular guess for a given exposure of a target is Star, the "group-guess" may be taken as Star,

* Several "letters to the editor," republished in abridged form from the *Journal of the* (London) *Society for Psychical Research, 36* (1951), 409–12, 452.

and the group is then treated statistically as an individual. The group opinion can be determined either at the time of the guess or after the session. Both methods demand extra time and work, though much of this can be saved by a resourceful experimenter. . . .

I would like to express the hope that in any future reports Dr. Schmeidler will state explicitly whether each result comes from individual or group experiments, and give rather more complete accounts of the procedure used for statistical evaluation.

CHRISTOPHER SCOTT

SIR,—Mr. Scott's criticism is technically justified. In the article to which he refers, probabilities were calculated from t-scores both for the individually tested subjects and for the group tests in which all members of a class guessed at the same targets. As he points out, this is not theoretically correct.

But does it matter, in practice? I should like to raise two points which indicate that it does not; and that the method which was used leads to the same conclusions as the correct but more time-consuming one devised by Dr. Greville.

The first is empirical. In several other series which were similar in procedure and in the nature of the target, both the Greville and other methods were applied, and no appreciable differences were found. Dr. Betty M. Humphrey [1949] states in relation to this: "In every case the CR of the difference obtained by the Greville method differed from that obtained by the binomial formula by only a few hundredths of a point. (For example, for Series S_1, S_2, S_3, CR's of the difference obtained by the binomial formula were 2.79, 2.81, 2.29. By Dr. Greville's method the comparable CR's of the difference were 2.76, 2.75, 2.26.)

"Because of the almost prohibitive amount of work involved in carrying out the extensive analyses according to the Greville method, and especially because of the fact that no appreciable difference has ever been found in connection with any of the series of this report between the results obtained by the Greville method and the simple binomial formula, it was deemed unnecessary to apply the Greville method to the series of the present report where the CR's obtained were not of borderline significance."

. . . Since [the probabilities quoted in my paper would not] ordinarily be considered borderline, I followed Dr. Humphrey's precedent in evaluating the data. Even allowing for some margin of error because of the statistical method used, we can, I think, take it that differences between the groups were demonstrated by the research. If this is so, spending many hours on further evaluation would not contribute to our understanding.

My second point relates to theory. The reason for applying a correction to multiple calls on a target is the possibility that many members of a group have a preferred pattern of symbol choice, which (if it exists) may be similar to, or different from the symbol pattern of the target list. This can, of course, affect the data when an experiment uses only one target list. In our case, however, 27 groups guessed at 9 lists each, making 243 lists in all.[1] It seems obvious that the importance of multiple calling is minimized when so many sets of multiple calls are used.

In this connection, Dr. Greville has written to me, "Experience has shown that similar stimulus preferences among the members of a group are an important factor only when (1) the number of possible stimuli from which the target is selected is very small, *and* (2) the number of calls in an experimental session is also very small."

Neither of these conditions was fulfilled in the research to which Mr. Scott refers; thus his criticism would seem to be inappropriate. . . .

GERTRUDE SCHMEIDLER

SIR,—Dr. Schmeidler is perfectly right, and except on the academic issue I was quite wrong. . . .

CHRISTOPHER SCOTT

1. The article under discussion summarizes only an early part of the data of this book. There were 37 group-testing sessions in all.

References

Allport, G. W., and Vernon, P. E. (1931) *A study of values*, Boston, Houghton Mifflin.

Anderson, M., and White, R. (1957) A further investigation of teacher-pupil attitudes and clairvoyance test results. *J. Parapsychol.*, *21*, 81–97.

Bevan, J. M. (1947) The relation of attitude to success in ESP scoring. *J. Parapsychol.*, *11*, 296–309.

Brend, W. A. (1941) Differential diagnosis of contusion of the brain and psychoneurosis. *Brit. med. J.*, *1*, 885–7.

Bridgman, P. W. (1956) Probability, logic, and ESP. *Science, 123*, 15–17.

Brown, G. S. (1953) Statistical significance in psychical research. *Nature, 172*, No. 4369, 154–6.

Brugmans, H. J. F. W., Heymans, G., and Weinberg, A. A. (1922) Une communication sur des experiences télépathiques au laboratoire de psychologie a Groningue. In *Compte rendu du Premier Congrès International des Recherches Psychiques*, Copenhagen, 396–408.

—— (1924) L'état passif d'un télépathe, contrôle par le phénomène psychogalvanique. In *II Congrès International*, Paris, Presses universitaires de France, 95–125.

Burdock, E. I. (1954) A case of ESP: Critique of "Personal values and ESP scores" by G. R. Schmeidler. *J. abn. soc. Psychol.*, *49*, 314–15.

Carington, W. (1944) Experiments on the paranormal cognition of drawings: III. Steps in the development of a repeatable technique. *Proc. Amer. Soc. psychic. Res.*, *24*, 1–107.

Casper, G. W. (1951) A further study of the relation of attitude to success in ESP scoring. *J. Parapsychol.*, *15*, 139–45.

Cass, W. A., and McReynolds, P. (1951) A contribution to Rorschach norms. *J. consult. Psychol.*, *15*, 178–84.

Denny-Brown, D. (1945) Cerebral concussion. *Physiol. Rev., 25*, 296–325.

Eccles, J. C. (1953) *The neurophysiological basis of mind*, London, Oxford University Press, 314 pp.

Ehrenwald, J. (1948) *Telepathy and medical psychology*, New York, W. W. Norton.

Eilbert, L., and Schmeidler, G. R. (1950) A study of certain psychological factors in relation to ESP performance. *J. Parapsychol.*, *14*, 53–74.

Fisher, R. A., and Yates, F. (1953) *Statistical tables for biological, agricultural, and medical research*, 4th ed. New York, Hafner Publishing Co.

Forwald, H. (1957) A continuation of the study of psychokinesis and physical conditions. *J. Parapsychol.*, *21*, 98–121.

Gerber, R., and Schmeidler, G. R. (1957) An investigation of relaxation and of acceptance of the experimental situation as related to ESP scores in maternity patients. *J. Parapyschol.*, *21*, 47–57.

Greenwood, J. A., and Stuart, C. E. (1937) Mathematical techniques used in ESP research. *J. Parapsychol.*, *1*, 206–25.

Grela, J. J. (1945) Effect on ESP scoring of hypnotically induced attitudes. *J. Parapsychol.*, *9*, 194–202.

GREVILLE, T. N. E. (1944) On multiple matching with one variable deck. *Ann. math. Statist., 15,* 432–4.

HUMPHREY, B. M. (1946) Success in ESP as related to form of response drawings. *J. Parapsychol., 10,* 78–106, 181–96.

—— (1949) Further work of Dr. Stuart on interest test ratings and ESP. *J. Parapsychol., 13,* 151–65.

KAHN, S. D. (1952) Studies in extrasensory perception: experiments utilizing an electronic scoring device. *Proc. Amer. Soc. psychic. Res., 25,* 1–48.

KENDALL, M. G. (1951) *The advanced theory of statistics, Vols. I & II,* 3d ed. London, Chas. Griffen and Co.

KLOPFER, B., and KELLEY, D. (1942) *The Rorschach technique,* Yonkers-on-Hudson, New York, World Book Co.

KLOPFER, B., AINSWORTH, M. D., KLOPFER, W. G., and HOLT, R. R. (1954) *Developments in the Rorschach technique, Vol. 1,* Yonkers-on-Hudson, New York, World Book Co.

LATIMER, W. M., and YOUNG, H. A. (1939) The nature of visual observations at low light intensities. *Physical Rev., 56,* 963–4.

MCCONNELL, R. A. (1954) A review of Soal and Bateman's *Modern experiments in telepathy. J. Parapsychol., 18,* 245–58.

—— (1956) The nature of the laboratory evidence for ESP. In *Extrasensory perception: A Ciba Foundation symposium,* London, J. and A. Churchill, Ltd.; Boston, Little, Brown & Co., pp. 4–13.

—— (1957) Psi phenomena and methodology. *Amer. Scientist, 45,* 125–36.

MEEHL, P. E., and SCRIVEN, M. (1956) Compatibility of science and ESP. *Science, 123,* 14–15.

MUNROE, R. L. (1945) *Prediction of the adjustment and academic performance of college students by a modification of the Rorschach method* (Appl. Psychol. Monog., No. 7), 104 pp.

NICOL, J. F., and HUMPHREY, B. M. (1953) The exploration of ESP and human personality. *J. Amer. Soc. psychic. Res., 47,* 133–78.

NOWLIS, V. (1958) On the use of drugs in the analysis of complex human behavior with emphasis on the study of mood. In *Current Trends in Methodology in Psychology,* Pittsburgh, University of Pittsburgh Press.

PEATMAN, J. G., and SCHAFER, R. (1942) A table of random numbers from selective service numbers. *J. Psychol., 14,* 295–305.

PRATT, J. G., and PRICE, M. M. (1938) The experimenter-subject relationship in tests for ESP. *J. Parapsychol., 2,* 84–94.

PRATT, J. G., and WOODRUFF, J. L. (1939) Size of stimulus symbols in extra-sensory perception. *J. Parapsychol., 3,* 121–58.

PRICE, G. R. (1955) Science and the supernatural. *Science, 122,* 359–67.

—— (1956) Where is the definitive experiment? *Science, 123,* 17–18.

RHINE, J. B. (1952) The problem of psi-missing. *J. Parapsychol., 16,* 90–129.

—— (1956a) Comments on "Science and the supernatural." *Science, 123,* 11–14.

—— (1956b) The experiment should fit the hypothesis. *Science, 123,* 19.

RHINE, J. B., and PRATT, J. G. (1954) A review of the Pearce-Pratt distance series of ESP tests. *J. Parapsychol., 18,* 165–77.

RIESS, B. F. (1937) A case of high scores in card guessing at a distance. *J. Parapsychol., 1,* 260–3 (see also *3,* 79–84).

RORSCHACH, H. (1942) *Psychodiagnostics,* New York, Grune and Stratton.

ROSENZWEIG, S. (1945) The picture-association method and its application in a study of reactions to frustration. *J. Personal., 14,* 3–23.

Rosenzweig, S., Clarke, H. J., Garfield, M. S., and Lehndorff, A. (1946) Scoring samples for the Rosenzweig Picture-Frustration Study. *J. Psychol.*, *21*, 45–72.

Rotter, J. B., Rafferty, J. E., and Schachtitz, E. (1949) Validation of the Rotter Incomplete Sentences Blank for College Screening. *J. consult. Psychol.*, *13*, 348–56.

Scherer, W. B. (1948) Spontaneity as a factor in ESP. *J. Parapsychol.*, *12*, 126–47.

Schmeidler, G. R. (1943a) Predicting good and bad scores in a clairvoyance experiment: a preliminary report. *J. Amer. Soc. psychic. Res.*, *37*, 103–10.

—— (1943b) Predicting good and bad scores in a clairvoyance experiment: a final report. *J. Amer. Soc. psychic. Res.*, *37*, 210–21.

—— (1947) Rorschach variables in relation to ESP scores. *J. Amer. Soc. psychic. Res.*, *41*, 35–64.

—— (1949) Comparison of ESP scores with Rorschachs scored by different workers. *J. Amer. Soc. psychic. Res.*, *43*, 94–7.

—— (1950a) ESP performance and the Rorschach test. *J.* (London) *Soc. psychic. Res.*, *35*, 323–39

—— (1950b) Some relations between picture-frustration ratings and ESP scores. *J. Personal.*, *18*, 331–43.

—— (1952a) Personal values and ESP scores. *J. abn. soc. Psychol.*, *47*, 757–61.

—— (1952b) Rorschachs and ESP scores of patients suffering from cerebral concussion. *J. Parapsychol.*, *16*, 80–9.

—— (1954) Picture-frustration ratings and ESP scores for subjects who showed moderate annoyance at the ESP task. *J. Parapsychol.*, *18*, 137–52.

Schmeidler, G. R., and Allison, L. W. (1948) A repetition of Carington's experiments with free drawings. *J. Amer. Soc. psychic. Res.*, *42*, 97–107.

Smith, K., and Canon, H. J. (1954) A methodological refinement in the study of ESP, and negative findings. *Science*, *120*, 148–9.

Soal, S. G. (1956) On "Science and the supernatural." *Science*, *123*, 9–11.

Soal, S. G., and Bateman, F. (1954) *Modern experiments in telepathy*, New Haven, Yale University Press; London, Faber and Faber.

Soal, S. G., and Goldney, K. M. (1943) Experiments in precognitive telepathy. *Proc.* (London) *Soc. psychic. Res.*, *47*, 21–150.

Thouless, R. H., and Wiesner, B. P. (1947) The psi processes in normal and paranormal psychology. *Proc.* (London) *Soc. psychic. Res.*, *48*, 177–96. Reprinted in *J. Parapsychol.*, *12* (1948), 192–212.

Tippett, L. H. C. (1927) *Random sampling numbers.* (Tracts for computers, No. XV), Cambridge University Press.

Van de Castle, R. L., and White, R. R. (1955) A report on a sentence completion form of sheep-goat attitude scale. *J. Parapsychol.*, *19*, 171–9.

Walter, W. G. (1953) *The living brain*, New York, W. W. Norton, 311 pp.

Wolfle, D. (1956) Extrasensory perception [editorial]. *Science*, *123*, 7.

Woodruff, J. L., and Dale, L. A. (1950) Subject and experimenter attitudes in relation to ESP scoring. *J. Amer. Soc. psychic. Res.*, *44*, 87–112.

INDEX